MW01062114

COMMANDING YOUR *Morning*

Daily

Devotional

CINDY TRIMM

CHARISMA HOUSE

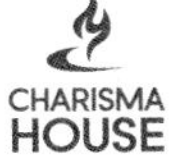

Most Charisma House Book Group products are available at special quantity discounts for bulk purchase for sales promotions, premiums, fund-raising, and educational needs. For details, write Charisma House Book Group, 600 Rinehart Road, Lake Mary, Florida 32746, or telephone (407) 333-0600.

Commanding Your Morning Daily Devotional
by Cindy Trimm
Published by Charisma House
Charisma Media/Charisma House Book Group
600 Rinehart Road
Lake Mary, Florida 32746
www.charismahouse.com

Cover design by Lisa Rae McClure
Design Director: Justin Evans

Visit the author's website at www.trimminternational.com.

Library of Congress Cataloging-in-Publication Data:
Trimm, Cindy.
Commanding your morning daily devotional / Cindy Trimm. -- First edition.
pages cm
ISBN 978-1-62136-609-6 (casebound) -- ISBN 978-1-62136-631-7 (e-book)
1. Devotional calendars. 2. Spiritual warfare--Prayers and devotions. I. Title.
BV4811.T75 2014
235'.4--dc23
2013038354

19 20 21 22 23 — 10 9 8 7
Printed in Canada

This is the beginning of a new day
You have been given this day to use as you
will.
You can waste it or use it for good.
What you do today is important
Because you are exchanging a day of your
life for it.
When tomorrow comes, this day will be
gone forever.
In its place is something that you have left
behind...
Let it be something good.

—Author Unknown

Introduction

Many people feel powerless to control their lives and circumstances. They know they're not getting everything they're supposed to get out of life, but they can't figure out why. What they don't realize is that life is not subject to chance. It doesn't have to be a mystery, and we don't have to walk through it powerless to change the direction we're headed. If we're not experiencing divine success and prosperity, we can do something about it.

In this daily devotional you will be empowered with a prayer strategy I call "Commanding Your Morning." Prior to every great kingdom event demonstrated by Jesus, the Bible indicates that He got alone with God and spent time in prayer. During those times Jesus was establishing God's divine agenda in the earth realm and downloading victory, success, and prosperity into His day while dislodging evil. He was commanding the morning and taking authority over His day.

To *command* means to:

- Instruct
- Dictate
- Exercise authority
- Master and conquer
- Control

- Give orders to
- Demand so as to receive what is due
- Rule
- Decree
- Supervise
- Keep watch
- Manage
- Administrate
- Regulate

Don't miss this principle. The power for change is in your mouth. The power for prosperity is in your mouth. The power for health and healing is in your mouth. The power for a successful ministry, marriage, business, relationship, or whatever you need is in your mouth! God has a plan for your personal world, but it depends on you fulfilling it by first taking control of your mind and your mouth. You must fill your thoughts and words with light and truth. We define our lives by our words and thoughts.

When you command your morning, you pull success from the spiritual realm into your day. When you command your morning, you give your reality divine assignments. You must be willing to declare and establish in the spirit realm today what you want to see manifested tomorrow.

In this context, morning does not solely refer to the hours registered on the face of a clock but to the period of time that exists before circumstances happen. You do not have to wait to get sick or experience financial loss or plummeting marriage relations before positioning and posturing yourself to pray. There are many situations in your life that can be prohibited through preemptive prayer.

In the New Testament we see the specific prayer strategy Jesus employed to command His mornings. Let's look at Matthew 14:23–32:

> And when He had sent the multitudes away, He went up on the mountain by Himself to pray. Now when evening came, He was alone there. But the boat was now in the middle of the sea, tossed by the waves, for the wind was contrary. Now in the fourth watch of the night Jesus went to them, walking on the sea. And when the disciples saw Him walking on the sea, they were troubled, saying, "It is a ghost!" And they cried out for fear. But immediately Jesus spoke to them, saying, "Be of good cheer! It is I; do not be afraid." And Peter answered Him

> and said, "Lord, if it is You, command me to come to You on the water." So He said, "Come." And when Peter had come down out of the boat, he walked on the water to go to Jesus. But when he saw that the wind was boisterous, he was afraid; and beginning to sink he cried out, saying, "Lord, save me!" And immediately Jesus stretched out His hand and caught him, and said to him, "O you of little faith, why did you doubt?" And when they got into the boat, the wind ceased.

Long before the enemy manifested himself by devising a storm, Jesus had programmed life, prosperity, and success into His day and into the lives of His disciples. The devil could not kill them or cause them to fail. Although they met with frustrating circumstances, they prevailed because Jesus had already paved the way to their success with His prayers.

This principle can be found in the Old Testament, as well. Job 38:12–13 reveals a conversation God had with Job. He asked a series of questions that exposes the principle of commanding the morning:

> Have you commanded the morning since
> your days began,
> And caused the dawn to know its place,

> That it might take hold of the ends of the
> earth,
> And the wicked be shaken out of it?

When you understand and implement this prayer strategy of commanding your morning, you will literally begin to experience what I call "overnight" success. When I say "overnight," I am referring once again to the power of the spoken word in relation to God's eternal plan for your life and your prayer posture relative to setting these plans into motion. What you decree forth before you go to bed at night and continue to declare as you rise in the morning will keep the spiritual world active all night long—while you sleep the peaceful sleep of the righteous! You will start your day with power and end it with blessing. Remember, when we refer to days, nights, and seasons, we are not referring to the time on a clock or a day on a calendar; we are referring to the timing of the Lord, which requires neither a clock nor a calendar. His timing for blessing is now, in the present moment, and is regulated by simple and continual acts of obedience (Deut. 28:1–2).

When you employ this strategy, you activate the twenty-four-hour anointing—an anointing that brings all the elements surrounding your life into divine alignment with God's purpose for you. This anointing brings you to a kind of prophetic critical mass. An example of this would be the life of Joseph. One night, after a long period of captivity, Joseph went to bed a felon, and he woke up positioned to be prime minister. All the elements of his life collided with purpose and exploded into a prophetic critical mass. There was nothing and no one who could stop his impending success and prosperity. When you command your morning, nothing and no one can hinder, alter, or abort your destiny.

Use this book to allow God to sit with you in conversation each day and to fill your spirit with His counsel and guidance. It will enrich your life and prepare you to be victorious in each circumstance and situation that you face. God's Word—whether written or whispered silently in your spirit—will be all you need to live a life that is fully pleasing to Him.

January

January 1

The Dawn of New Possibilities

Therefore glorify the Lord *in the dawning light.*
—Isaiah 24:15

Every new day with God brings the dawn of new and better possibilities. Today could turn out to be the best day of your life—but how it ends largely depends on how you begin it. You are in charge of taking control of your day from its very beginning—as you command your morning—and as you do, know that whatever begins with God has to end right. No matter how good or bad your life is, every circumstance can change for the best if you learn how to command your morning before your day begins.

Father, I stand and declare that today is a new day. Every element of my day shall cooperate with Your purpose and destiny for me. Anything or anyone assigned to undermine, frustrate, hinder, or hurt me, I command to be moved out of my sphere of influence. I greet today with great anticipation of the good things You have prepared for me. In Jesus's name, amen.

January 2

Speak It Into Being

Let there be...
—Genesis 1

Eons ago, with neither fanfare nor audience, the mighty Creator of the universe spoke. His utterance would constitute the first recorded words. God thought, then spoke, and the universe came into being. God spoke out what He had seen in His mind as He had dreamed about creating the universe, and when He spoke, the earth, all the planets, the sun, moon, and stars, as well as every plant, animal, and humanity itself, appeared just as He had seen us all in His mind's eye. God spoke, and from seemingly "nothingness" came everything that exists in the physical universe.

Lord, You spoke the worlds into existence, and You put the power of life and death within my tongue. So I speak life over my day. Let Your Holy Spirit and His wisdom, understanding, and prophetic insight be upon me today. Grant me the ability to hear clearly as You give me creative ideas to be more fruitful and productive. Open my ears and let Your Word inspire me to righteousness. In Jesus's name, amen.

January 3

All Will Be Revealed

[God] will bring to light the things now hidden in darkness and will disclose the purposes of the heart.
—1 Corinthians 4:5, esv

Everything in the universe begins with and revolves around two things: *words* and *thoughts*. Our thoughts, intentions, motivations, and aspirations—whether they be secretly pondered in the heart, openly declared as desires, or formally written as goals—mold and shape our personal universe into something that is either grand and beautiful or base and hideous. Whatever you harbor in the innermost corridors of your thought life will, sooner or later, reveal itself in the outer arena through your words or actions. Whatever is hidden will eventually be brought to light. Just as a seed is for a time hidden under the ground, it will eventually break through the surface, and its true essence will be revealed.

Father, I commit to fill my mouth with Your Word. Let it renew my mind and make me more like You. Weed out everything in my heart that is not like You. Make me more like You! Cause my will to work in harmony with Yours. I break evil and inappropriate thought patterns in my mind. Let the words of my mouth and the meditations of my heart be acceptable in Your sight. In Jesus's name, amen.

January 4

God Has Your Success

For I know the thoughts that I think toward you, says the Lord, thoughts of peace and not of evil, to give you a future and a hope.
—Jeremiah 29:11

Life does not have to be a mystery for you. You do not have to grope mindlessly in the dark for the right path through life. God already has your success, prosperity, and fulfillment all planned out; you just have to follow His directions to find it. You can take control of your life and experience divine success and prosperity by following God's directions outlined in His Word. He has a wonderful plan for you—and His plan for your personal world depends on you first taking control of your mind and your mouth. Learn to fill your thoughts and words with light and truth.

Father, thank You for having such good plans for me. You have deposited into me all I need to fulfill Your purpose. I release into this day the vision, direction, creativity, and resourcefulness You have placed within me. Synchronize my life with Your perfect timing. Let everything about this day cooperate with Your purpose and plan. In Jesus's name, amen.

January 5

Live in the Light

He rescued us from the domain of darkness, and transferred us to the kingdom of His beloved Son.
—Colossians 1:13, nas

The Bible tells us we can reside in a spiritual realm characterized by happiness, empowered living, success, and prosperity. Through a relationship with God we are miraculously conveyed into the kingdom of light—a realm that opens unlimited doors of opportunity, enabling us to discover our divine purpose, maximize our best potential, and experience boundless abundance.

Light is not only the absence of darkness, but it is also the yoke-breaking presence of God, the liberating essence of truth, and the mind-transforming potential of every revelation of God. It is all that is good within and among us.

Father, let me be even more aware of Your presence in my life today. I will not fear new challenges that present themselves today because I know You are with me. You take my hand and lead me when I don't know the way; You turn darkness into light and make the rough places smooth (Isa. 42:16). You are worthy of my total trust, and I put complete confidence in You. In Jesus's name, amen.

January 6

You Have All You Need

His divine power has given to us all things that pertain to life and godliness, through the knowledge of Him who called us by glory and virtue, by which have been given to us exceedingly great and precious promises, that through these you may be partakers of the divine nature.
—2 Peter 1:3–4

God, in His infinite wisdom, has already given us all things pertaining to life that we might partake of His divine nature. Included in this celestial equipping are divine thoughts and inspired words. As a spiritual being created in the image of God (Gen. 1:26), your spiritual genes hold the creative power to frame your personal world by the thoughts and words you think and speak, which are divine tools given for your creative use. All you are, experience, and ultimately achieve can be traced back to how you have made use of these two simple yet vastly powerful tools—your words and thoughts.

Lord, the preparation belongs to man but the ends of the tongue belong to You. Give me the tongue of the learned. Let my words be more than motivation; let them carry life. Open my eyes to see prophetic revelation in Your Word. Cause me to break through any roadblocks that would hinder me from receiving from You. Let Your Word renew my mind. Amen.

January 7

The Power of Words

For as [a man or woman] thinks in his heart, so is he.
—Proverbs 23:7

The power of the spoken word is one of life's greatest mysteries. All you will ever be or accomplish hinges on how you choose to govern what comes out of your mouth. By what you allow to occupy your mind and mouth, you can either bless your life to great heights of success or send it orbiting into realms of failure, sadness, and discontentment. This is why Proverbs urges, "Guard your heart above all else, for it determines the course of your life" (Prov. 4:23, NLT). Jesus followed suit by declaring, "For whatever is in your heart determines what you say. A good person produces good things from the treasury of a good heart, and an evil person produces evil things from the treasury of an evil heart" (Matt. 12:34–35, NLT).

Lord, set a guard over my lips today and search my heart. Try me and know my thoughts. See if there is any evil way in me and lead me in the way everlasting (Ps. 139:23–24). If there is anything in my life that displeases You, Father, remove it in Jesus's name. Circumcise my heart, and cause my desires and my words to line up with Yours. In Jesus's name, amen.

January 8

Reap What You Sow

For they sow the wind, and they shall reap the whirlwind.
—Hosea 8:7, ESV

What occupies your mind determines what eventually fills your mouth. Your outer world showcases all that has dominated—and at times subjugated—your inner world. Are you aware of the true meaning of the things you are speaking out? As the prophet Hosea remarked, each one of us must take responsibility for what we experience in life. We are the sum total of every choice we have ever made or let happen. If you do not like where you are, you are only one thought away from turning toward the life you desire.

Father, make me more aware of the power of my words today. I declare that my season of frustration is over. As I guard my tongue, my life is changing for the best. In the name of Jesus I declare that everything this season should bring to me must come forth. Every invisible barrier must be destroyed. I declare that I am a prophetic trailblazer. I am taking new territory spiritually, emotionally, relationally, and professionally. I decree and declare that You are opening doors no man could open, and I am advancing in my prophetic destiny. In the name of Jesus, amen.

January 9

Master Your Thoughts

I will put my instructions deep within them,
and I will write them on their hearts.
—Jeremiah 31:33, NLT

It is paramount that you become the master of your thoughts. Sift your thought life. Filter out anything you don't want to have show up in your future, and focus on what you truly desire. God wired your thoughts to have power so you would be equipped to overcome every obstacle. He fashioned you to create, innovate, strategize, and succeed—and just to be sure, He put His own divine thoughts and nature within you. Hook up your heart with the ultimate power source.

Lord, I surrender my thoughts to You. Teach me to love You with all my heart and all my mind. I commit to set my affection on things above, not things on the earth. I limit myself when I rely on my own wisdom. Your thoughts and Your ways are so much higher than mine. I can only honor You with my words if I allow You to change my mind. So I release You to move in my life. Transform my thinking with Your Word. I declare that I will not lean on my own understanding, no matter how tempting it may be, but I will abide in Your truth. In Jesus's name, amen.

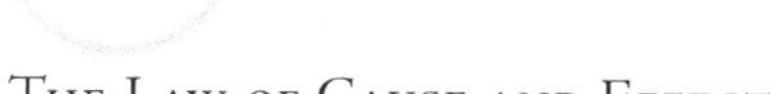

January 10

The Law of Cause and Effect

He who sows sparingly will also reap sparingly, and he who sows bountifully will also reap bountifully.
—2 Corinthians 9:6

Because the law of cause and effect is continually at work, there is always an inner cause for every outer effect. Your outer world is a direct result of your inner world. Every circumstance in life is a result of a choice—and every choice is the result of a thought. All those things that fill your mind hold the keys to your reality. Your thoughts provide the fuel for your words, and your words provide the fuel for your world.

Lord, according to Your Word, I declare that my thoughts are governed only by "things true, noble, reputable, authentic, compelling, gracious—the best, not the worst; the beautiful, not the ugly; things to praise, not things to curse" (Phil. 4:8–9, The Message). I will not forget Your ways or forsake mercy and truth. As a result, my day will be filled with peace, and I will find favor with God and man (Prov. 3:1–4). In the name of Jesus, amen.

January 11

You Live a Spiritual Existence

These things we also speak, not in words which man's wisdom teaches but which the Holy Spirit teaches, comparing spiritual things with spiritual.
—1 Corinthians 2:13

The temporal realm has its roots in the spiritual. Grabbing hold of this profound spiritual truth will enable you to make critical connections that can transform your life. Once you understand that the spiritual realm is the "causal realm," you will begin to grasp the massive power of your thoughts, ideas, words, and prayers—spiritual things that engineer, mold, and craft the current and future state of your temporal existence.

Father, I choose to walk by faith and not by sight. I miss out on Your best for me when I follow my own way. I decree and declare that today begins a new season. Old things are gone. Frustration and failure are part of my past. You are making all things new. I decree and declare that I now walk in success and prosperity. Anything or anyone assigned to undermine or hinder God's plans and purposes must move out of my way in Jesus's name. Father, I declare that I am Yours and I am led by Your hand. In Jesus's name, amen.

Your Thoughts Are a Magnetic Field

Fix your thoughts on what is true, and honorable, and right, and pure, and lovely, and admirable. Think about things that are excellent and worthy of praise.
—Philippians 4:8, NLT

Your thoughts and words are transmitted like a shortwave radio signal. They send messages out on a specific frequency and are transmitted back to you as an experience or occurrence in your life. Your thoughts create something like a magnetic field around you, while your words provide a kind of spiritual homing device that attracts either positive people, things, and experiences or negative people, things, and experiences. Therefore, you must learn to fill your mind with good, godly, and great thoughts. What you think has the power to literally transform your life.

Father, I take my thoughts captive today and submit them to You. Every argument and lofty opinion raised against the knowledge of God I destroy. I know that it is what comes out of my mouth that defiles me, so I speak life and truth. I love You, Lord, with all my heart and all my mind (Matt. 22:37). Place upon me Samuel's anointing for sensitivity and obedience to the voice of God as I stand in complete agreement with Your Word. In Jesus's name, amen.

January 13

Commanding Light in the Darkness

Let there be light.
—Genesis 1:3

Sometimes when concepts are difficult to grasp, you simply need to say, "Let there be light!" This was the first recorded thing God said. Light illuminates. What you really want is for your spirit and your mind to be illuminated—you want to obtain insight and wisdom. When it feels as if you are wandering in the dark and can't figure out what to do, stop and command, "Let there be light!"

Lord, let there be light! Illuminate Your Word. Give me a spirit of wisdom and revelation. All-powerful God, place Your anointing upon me. Place on me Solomon's anointing for resource management, wisdom, wealth, success, and prosperity; Isaac's anointing for investment strategies; Cyrus's anointing for financial acumen; Esther's anointing for divine favor and kingdom strategies; and Daniel's anointing for government, excellence, and integrity. Let the anointing on my life flow uncontaminated and unhindered. Let it repel every individual with a diabolical assignment. Let the anointing that is on my life for this season attract only those divinely ordained to assist me in fulfilling my assignment in the earth. In the name of Jesus, amen.

Be Vigilant

He who walks righteously and speaks uprightly... who stops his ears from hearing of bloodshed and shuts his eyes from looking on evil, he will dwell on the heights; his place of defense will be the fortresses of rocks; his bread will be given him; his water will be sure.

—Isaiah 33:15–16, esv

It is essential that you become extremely vigilant about what enters your mind daily. What you hear affects how you think and what you believe. If you want to have life-affirming thoughts—thoughts of success and prosperity—then fill your ears with words that will produce these things in your life. Eventually, if you hear something enough, over time it will form a belief, and that belief will produce a corresponding action. It is this hearing—and hearing again—that is the impetus of faith.

Faith comes by hearing and hearing by the Word of God. Open my ears today to hear Your truth. My faith does not rest in men's wisdom but in Your power (1 Cor. 2:5). I do not mind the things of the flesh but things of the Spirit. Because I walk according to the Spirit and not the flesh, I bear the fruit of the Spirit: love, joy, peace, longsuffering, gentleness, goodness, meekness, temperance, and faith. I will not be moved by circumstances. I walk by faith and not by sight. In the name of Jesus, amen.

January 15

Faith Comes by Hearing

So faith comes from hearing, and hearing through the word of Christ.
—Romans 10:17, esv

Jesus Christ, a kingdom practitioner, knew the power of truth combined with the principle of faith. He knew that faith came by hearing, so He spent hours teaching and dialoguing with His disciples. He taught His students success principles derived from spiritual laws in order to build their faith in their ability to make a difference in the world. He began the arduous task of transforming the mind-sets of twelve outcasts and fishermen. He spoke many spiritual truths to them in order to stretch their paradigms of success and prosperity beyond the temporal, three-dimensional realm. He knew it would take constant exposure to the light for the light to finally turn on in them.

Father, stretch me. Enlarge my understanding of Your will and Your ways. Let the disciples' anointing for learning be upon me today. I let go of my preconceived opinions, doctrines, and beliefs, and I sit myself down in the school of the Holy Spirit. Help me grow in my knowledge of You. Open my heart and mind to receive Your truth. In Jesus's name, amen.

January 16

You Can Have Perfection

Every good gift and every perfect gift is from above, and comes down from the Father of lights, with whom there is no variation or shadow of turning.
—James 1:17

God wants you to have what is good and perfect. Did you get that? You don't just have to have good health; you can have *perfect* health. You don't have to settle for a good job; you can have a *perfect* job—or better still, the perfect business that not only pays the bills but also gives you enough left over to be a tremendous blessing to others. You don't have to settle for a good marriage; you can have the *perfect* marriage. You don't have to settle for a good life; you can have a *perfect* life. So go ahead—shout it from the rooftops: "Let there be light!" You will be delightfully surprised that perhaps what you have been looking for is right before your eyes. It was simply awaiting illumination.

Father, illuminate Your goodness to me today. You are a good Father who gives good gifts to Your children. Marvelous are Your works. You used all Your divine skill to put me together, and I am fearfully and wonderfully made. I declare that principalities and powers have no right to touch my life in any way, for I am in covenant with God and hidden in the secret place of the Most High. Amen.

January 17

You Have Access to God's Secrets

The knowledge of the secrets of the kingdom of heaven has been given to you, but not to them. Whoever has will be given more, and he will have an abundance. Whoever does not have, even what he has will be taken from him. This is why I speak to them in parables.

—Matthew 13:10–13, niv

Did you get that? As long as information remains a secret, hidden in obscurity, no one can prosper from it, no matter how powerful the secret or how mighty the person. But that person to whom it is made known—no matter who they are—will have access to abundance, and to whom it is not revealed, even that which this person has shall be taken away.

Father, You are the revealer of secrets. Give me supernatural insight today that allows me to more effectively walk out the calling on my life. Download fresh ideas that empower me to work more efficiently. Fill my mind with witty ideas and divine revelation that cause me to positively impact my family, workplace, church, community, and region. In the name of Jesus let everything prepared for me before the foundation of the world be released in its correct time and season. No substitutes, no setbacks, and no delays. Your kingdom come and Your will be done. In Jesus's name, amen.

January 18

Examine Your Thoughts

Gird up the loins of your mind.
—1 Peter 1:13

When you pursue knowledge, wisdom, and truth, your mouth will speak words out of that abundance that will frame your world. Make it a habit to examine what your thoughts are chasing after and what your words are gathering to you. Remember, the world within not only colors the world without, but it is also its blueprint. Be intentional about what you hear, how you think, and what you speak—for you are setting the stage for the reality you experience.

Father, I wear the helmet of salvation to protect my mind from negative thoughts that would derail Your purposes and plans for me. Truth protects my integrity, righteousness protects my reputation, the gospel of peace guides my every step, the shield of faith secures my future and destiny, and the sword of the Spirit grants me dominion and authority. I decree and declare a prophetic upgrading of my thought life. I cancel the effect of negative, self-defeating thought processes and patterns and put them under my feet. In the name of Jesus, amen.

January 19

You've Been Given Mysteries

To you it has been given to know the mystery of the kingdom of God.
—Mark 4:11

Everyone loves to be in on a secret. One of the worst things is feeling left out when it comes to being "in the know"—as if everyone is aware of something vitally important except for you. But worse than that is the feeling that there are important things everyone should know but few do. The Bible calls these types of secrets *mysteries*. For most people life is exactly that, a mystery. But Jesus came to help us solve our mysteries. He came to give us knowledge of the truth.

Father, open the eyes of my understanding and reveal Your mysteries to me. Give me new strategies for dealing with the challenges I face. Guide me into all truth as I keep my eyes on You. Download prophetic insight so that my prayers will be strategic. I want more than feel-good prayers; I want my mouth to speak life into my circumstances, my day, and my future. Renew my mind with the water of Your Word. I want to become more like You. In the name of Jesus, amen.

Seek Knowledge and Wisdom

Get wisdom! Get understanding! Do not forget, nor turn away from the words of my mouth.... Wisdom is the principal thing; therefore get wisdom. And in all your getting, get understanding.
—Proverbs 4:5–7

The key to victory in Christ—and in this life—is the knowledge and wisdom that unlock the mysteries of life. That is why God wants you to pursue wisdom and understanding above all else. Seek to know and understand how and why God has created you. This is one secret you can be in on! There is overcoming power in knowing it is God's desire for you to succeed and prosper, as well as knowing how He has designed you to create success and abundance in every sphere you influence.

Father, open my eyes to see my gifts and abilities the way You see them. I come against every limiting belief now in the name of Jesus. I release the will of God into my life and into my day. Let the power of the Holy Spirit overshadow me. Teach me Your ways, Lord, so that I may conduct my affairs in the most discerning, expeditious, and fiscally wise manner. Father, allow only those with divine assignments to be drawn to me. Let the light of Your Word illuminate my path and open divine gates of access to new doors of opportunity. In the name of Jesus, amen.

January 21

Begin to Imagine

Such knowledge is too wonderful for me;
it is high, I cannot attain it.
—Psalm 139:6

Dave Thomas, the founder of Wendy's, was raised by adoptive parents. As a child he always imagined one day owning a hamburger restaurant, and on November 15, 1969, the first Wendy's Old Fashioned Hamburgers opened. Dave Thomas personifies the principle that if you can see it in your mind first, you can achieve it.

So, my friend, the secret is out. It is your time to consciously paint the canvas of your life with whatever you aspire to achieve. Fill your mind with majestic thoughts. Generate excitement and expectation with every word that proceeds from your mouth. I urge you to create a masterpiece out of your life. Dare to imagine!

Father, remind me of the dreams You placed into my heart. I speak to those things that have died prematurely and declare today that they must live. Just as the dry bones came back together when Ezekiel called them forth, I declare that the dead pieces of my destiny will live again. Dead vision, dead strategies, dead alliances must live. I decree and declare that You are making all things new and my best days are yet to come. In Jesus's name, amen.

Fight With Your Mind and Mouth

Our struggle is not against flesh and blood, but against the rulers, against the authorities, against the powers of this dark world and against the spiritual forces of evil in the heavenly realms. Therefore put on the full armor of God, so that when the day of evil comes, you may be able to stand your ground.
—Ephesians 6:12–13, niv

You must learn to harness the power of your thoughts if you are to effectively reign as a king and priest on this earth. You must understand that you are a child of God and His representative in the earth. As such, He has given you power, authority, and dominion to overcome adversities. Your fight is not with flesh and blood but with powers and principalities. Such a fight can't be won with your hands but only with your mind and mouth. You must become as skilled in your thoughts and speech as a swordsman is with his sword. Taking control of your thoughts will cause you to gain control over your life. That is what putting on the armor of God is all about.

Father, the weapons of my warfare are not carnal, but they are mighty through God to the pulling down of strongholds. I remind principalities and powers that they have no right to touch my life, for I am in covenant with You. I am more than a conqueror, and I declare that my life is marked by victory not defeat, success and not failure. In Jesus's name, amen.

January 23

Win the Battle in Your Mind

For the weapons of our warfare are not of the flesh but have divine power to destroy strongholds. We destroy arguments and every lofty opinion raised against the knowledge of God, and take every thought captive to obey Christ.
—2 Corinthians 10:4–5, esv

Throughout the New Testament we are told that our battles do not take place in the temporal realm but in the spiritual realm. In nearly every book of the New Testament we are told to "not be afraid; only believe" (Mark 5:36), "gird up the loins of your mind" (1 Pet. 1:13), renew your mind (Rom. 12:2), and put on "the mind of Christ" (1 Cor. 2:16). We are taught in Romans that "to set the mind on the flesh is death, but to set the mind on the Spirit is life and peace" (Rom. 8:6, esv). We are instructed to take every thought captive. Every battle is won or lost in the arena of your mind.

According to Philippians 4:8, I declare that my thoughts are governed only by things true, noble, reputable, authentic, compelling, gracious—the best, not the worst; the beautiful, not the ugly; things to praise, not things to curse. Father, renew my mind with Your Word. Cause it to transform my thoughts so that my speech is in perfect alignment with what Your Word says I can do and be. In Jesus's name, amen.

January 24

Fear Can Cripple You

We seemed to ourselves like grasshoppers, and so we seemed to them.
—Numbers 13:33, ESV

One of the most heartbreaking stories of the Old Testament is told in Numbers when the Israelites disobeyed God by refusing to take possession of the land He had prepared for them. Because they saw themselves as small and weak—they believed in their own minds that they were as grasshoppers before giants—they were unable to fulfill God's call. The giants, who themselves had been afraid of the children of Israel, were instead empowered because of the Israelites' fear.

Father, I refuse to let fear keep me from what You have for me today. I am open to new opportunities. I walk through open doors. I will not be afraid of new challenges that present themselves because You are guiding me with Your hand and leading me into Your perfect will. I refuse to receive the negative words of the accuser. I will repeat only what You say about me. I have the mind of Christ and therefore seek things above and not beneath. In Jesus's name, amen.

January 25

Speak No Idle Word

Every idle word men may speak, they will give account of it in the day of judgment.
—Matthew 12:36

Too many people release careless words into the atmosphere and can't figure out why the life God has promised them isn't happening the way they hoped it would. Scripture has revealed to us that everything in the universe has to adjust itself to accommodate our words—good or bad, purposeful or errant. (See Proverbs 13:3; 18:21; 21:23.) Words with no kingdom assignment will be brought into judgment. You will be held accountable for every idle word, but you will also be rewarded for every faith-filled word.

Let the words of my mouth and the meditations of my heart be acceptable in Your sight, oh, Lord, my strength and my redeemer. I will let no corrupt communication proceed out of my mouth but only that which is edifying. I decree and declare a prophetic upgrading of my speech and thought life. I cancel the effect of negative, self-defeating words and thought processes, and I put them under my feet. I declare new cycles of victory, success, and prosperity will replace old cycles of failure, poverty, and death in my life. In the name of Jesus, amen!

January 26

Meditate on God's Word

This Book of the Law shall not depart from your mouth, but you shall meditate in it day and night, that you may observe to do according to all that is written in it. For then you will make your way prosperous, and then you will have good success. Have I not commanded you? Be strong and of good courage; do not be afraid, nor be dismayed, for the Lord your God is with you wherever you go.

—Joshua 1:8–9

God gave very specific instructions to Joshua about how to secure success, prosperity, and victory over every adversary. He instructed Joshua to meditate on His Word day and night so it would fill his heart, mind, and mouth. Then He commanded Joshua to be strong and courageous. Do you see the connection? Until his mind and mouth only thought and spoke God's Word, Joshua could not have any hope of being strong and of good courage. Right from the outset God made it a priority to address the issue of Joshua's mind—no other instructions or strategies took precedence over what occupied Joshua's thoughts.

In the name of Jesus I decree and declare that I have a cutting-edge, kingdom mentality that grants me new ways of thinking, working, and living. Since Your Word is a lamp unto my feet I will neither stumble nor fall. I am excited; my spirit is ignited; I walk in favor with God and man. In Jesus's name, amen.

January 27

Take Possession of Your Thoughts

Casting down arguments and every high thing that exalts itself against the knowledge of God, bringing every thought into captivity to the obedience of Christ.
—2 Corinthians 10:4–5

The first thing you must do in taking possession of all God has prepared for you is to take possession of your thoughts. You may not think this requires a great deal of effort, let alone training or practice, but there is only one thing harder to master than your thoughts, and that is your tongue! (See James 3:8.) Winning the battle in your thought life requires meditating daily on the truths found in Scripture, studying diligently to show yourself approved, and becoming an earnest and lifelong student of the art of spiritual warfare.

I study to show myself approved unto God, a workman who need not be ashamed, rightly dividing the Word of truth. Your Word is nigh unto me. It is in my mouth and in my heart that I may do it. I meditate on Your truth, that I may know Your ways and the path I should follow. I put my confidence in You. I declare that I will walk in Your favor and blessing as I diligently keep Your commandments and follow Your ways. In the name of Jesus, amen.

Wield the Two-Edged Sword

For the word of God is living and powerful, and sharper than any two-edged sword, piercing even to the division of soul and spirit, and of joints and marrow, and is a discerner of the thoughts and intents of the heart.
—Hebrews 4:12

You have the Word made flesh—the Spirit of Christ—residing in you. You have been given the name above every name as your spiritual authority, and you have a two-edged sword, which is the Word of God, at your disposal. Do you see how important God's Word is? All things are possible to those who believe (Mark 9:23), but without knowledge of the Word, you don't have the correct truths to believe.

I hide Your Word in my heart that I might not sin against You. All the promises of God are yes and amen in You, so I declare Your promises over my life. I declare that I walk in dominion and authority. My life is characterized by liberty. There is no slackness in my hand. Where I stand, God gives me the land. Thank You for crowning me with Your love and mercy and for satisfying me with all good things. In Jesus's name, amen.

January 29

Renew Your Mind

Do not be conformed to this world, but be transformed by the renewing of your mind, so that you may prove what the will of God is, that which is good and acceptable and perfect.
—Romans 12:2, NAS

How do you renew your mind? Through knowledge of the truth regarding who you are in Christ. If you were to build your life like a house of faith, knowledge of God would be its foundation, while knowledge of who you are in Christ would be its frame. If you do not take control of your inner thoughts, you will become a slave to your outer circumstances. You won't be driving your life; the storms and changing weather will.

Father, I know who I am in You. I am forgiven of my sins and redeemed by Your blood. I am filled with Your Holy Spirit and free from the power of darkness. I am more than a conqueror. I am fearfully and wonderfully made and the apple of Your eye. Thank You for blessing me with all spiritual blessings in heavenly places. You have made me complete in You, lacking absolutely nothing. Because of who You are, I have everything I need for life and godliness. In Jesus's name, amen.

Be Conscious of Your Thoughts

Summing it all up, friends, I'd say you'll do best by filling your minds and meditating on things true, noble, reputable, authentic, compelling, gracious—the best, not the worst; the beautiful, not the ugly; things to praise, not things to curse.... Do that, and God, who makes everything work together, will work you into his most excellent harmonies.
—Philippians 4:8–9, The Message

It is critically important to stay conscious of what's going on in your mind. Random thoughts lead to random accomplishments that rarely build upon one another. You are the sum total of your thoughts. Make sure you are grounding your beliefs and basing your faith on God's "rich life"—not some counterfeit, but the abundance of His kingdom—by filling your heart and mind with life-giving, biblical truth.

Father, enlighten the eyes of my heart that I may know the riches of the glory of Your inheritance. I refuse to stand in agreement with the enemy. I walk in freedom because I walk in the truth. I declare that I have the mind of Christ. I will dwell on things above and not things on the earth. The weapons of my warfare are specially designed to pull down every thought that would exalt itself against the knowledge of God. I declare that I am blessed today because I put my trust in You. In Jesus's name, amen.

January 31

Unlock God's Secrets for You

They are darkened in their understanding, alienated from the life of God because of the ignorance that is in them.
—Ephesians 4:18, esv

Don't be left out in the dark as an exile estranged from the good life God has for you. Do not be among those who perish for lack of knowledge (Hosea 4:6). Instead, be "in the know," unlock God's secrets for you, and get in on the good life. As you follow God's specific instructions and fill your thoughts with those things the Bible tells you to, you will discover that the world will begin to unfold before you with an array of possibilities and reflect back what you choose to focus upon.

Eye has not seen nor ear heard the things You have prepared for me. I choose to focus on things that are true, noble, right, and pure; things that are lovely, excellent, or praiseworthy. You keep me in perfect peace because I keep my mind on You. You used all Your divine skill to put me together, and You know me well. Give me a deeper revelation of what You have equipped me to do. I want all You have for me. Your kingdom is my priority, and Your assignment is my pleasure. Father, bring me into the fullness of all You have for me. In Jesus's name, amen.

February

February 1

Seeing Is Believing

And the Lord said, Behold, they are one people and they have all one language; and this is only the beginning of what they will do, and now nothing they have imagined they can do will be impossible for them.
—Genesis 11:6, amp

Thoughts are spiritual, and so is the inspirational process. Man begins with a concept in his mind—something he believes he is able to accomplish. He joins his will and intellect to his imagination, and then expectation sees it through. In Genesis 11 the people thought to themselves they could build a tower to heaven, and because they saw this tower in their minds, they were able to build it. God stopped them by causing confusion and making it impossible for them to communicate because the tower became an idol for them. However, this story still illustrates the power of our thoughts and words.

Father, I align my will with Your will, my thoughts with Your thoughts. I command everything that is misaligned to line up with Your purposes and plans. I want what You desire for me. Your plans are good. You want to prosper me and not harm me, to bring me hope and a future. Fill me with the knowledge of Your will that I may live a life worthy of You and that I may please You in every way. In Jesus's name, amen.

February 2

The Power of Imagination

Let the words of my mouth and the meditation of my heart be acceptable in your sight, O Lord, my rock and my redeemer.
—Psalm 19:14, esv

Imagination is the natural product of meditation. Life's opportunities and creativity diminish or explode based on your ability to harness your imagination. Albert Einstein said, "I am enough of an artist to draw freely upon my imagination. Imagination is more important than knowledge. Knowledge is limited. Imagination encircles the world."[1] If we can think of imagination as a door that opens to a world of possibilities, then intentions and the corresponding actions are the keys that unlock that door.

Father, let my imagination be inspired by Your Holy Spirit. Cause me to have prophetic visions and dreams, and let divine strategy accompany them so I will know how to make those dreams a reality. As I seek You, Father, tell me great and hidden things that I have not known (Jer. 33:3). Thank You for revealing Your thoughts to me. You have filled me with Your Spirit and given me the skill, intelligence, and knowledge to accomplish Your will. I will not make You small in my eyes, Lord, because I know that with You nothing is impossible. In Jesus's name, amen.

February 3

You Can Change Your Destiny

Stand your ground.... Stay alert and be persistent in your prayers.
—Ephesians 6:14–18, nlt

Do not be a victim. Call the shots and change your destiny. Be proactive and decisive as you declare God's Word over your life. God has given you the promise that whatsoever you declare in Jesus's name will be done (John 14:13–14), so you can be all He intended you to be on the earth—a shining example of God's goodness and love.

Father, there is more to me than meets the eye. You made me above and not beneath, the head and not the tail, and I will not live beneath my potential. In the name of Jesus I destroy every limiting belief that has taken root in my mind. I take authority over all destiny-altering activity. I break out of every form of bondage: emotional, psychological, financial, and spiritual. I will not let fear keep me from my destiny. I decree and declare that I will do everything You created me to do. Father, redeem the time the canker worm has eaten. Let every gift and calling You have deposited within me be released in its perfect time. In Jesus's name, amen.

Joined to the Spirit

It is the spirit in man, the breath of the Almighty, that makes him understand.
—Job 32:8, esv

God conceived and by His Spirit spoke into existence all that is. He brought what already existed in the spiritual into the temporal by the power of His Word. He breathed that creative force—His very Spirit—into humanity. It is His Spirit in you that gives inspiration and understanding of what already exists in the spiritual realm. That spirit in you has always existed—it is eternal—and it is the source of all revelation and inspiration. God's Spirit creates a blueprint in the form of understanding, and from that blueprint all things come to be.

Father, You sculpted me from nothing, and I carry the marks of Your great design. I am well prepared to accomplish every task that awaits me today. Lord, You have given me creativity, ingenuity, wisdom, a strong work ethic, and a disciplined mind. In the name of Jesus I decree and declare that You are enlarging my borders and everything about me is changing for the best. I declare that my mind is fortified and resolute. My emotions are sound and stable. My faith is steadfast and unfaltering. I am Your child, O God, and You cause me to overcome. In the name of Jesus, amen.

February 5

Inspired Into Being

But you are not in the flesh but in the Spirit, if indeed the Spirit of God dwells in you.
—Romans 8:9

Before we had the computer, certain people saw a necessity for it and were inspired. This inspiration came out of the realm of the spirit. From the computer to symphonies to cures for cancer, everything started as an inspiration. All good inspiration comes from God. He is the Great Inspirer and the Almighty Enabler. All things are possible to those who put their trust in Him.

Father, open my spiritual eyes and ears to pick up Your revelation knowledge. I will not turn away from Your voice when you speak to me. I desire greater discernment. Open my ears to hear Your witty ideas and creative inventions. Cause me to see new tactics and strategies that allow me to blaze trails in my field. As I advance into new realms spiritually, professionally, and/or socially, let me not be seduced by the spirit of covetousness or the pride of life. Father, let me pursue only what You desire for me. In the name of Jesus, amen.

His Thoughts Toward You Are Good

Now to him who is able to do exceedingly abundantly above all that we ask or think, according to the power that works in us, to Him be glory in the church by Christ Jesus to all generations, forever and ever.
—Ephesians 3:20–21

Inspiration is a God thing. Inspiration is God Himself speaking into the human spirit. Inspirational thoughts are God finding expression for His will through the minds of human beings. According to Jeremiah 29:11, God's thoughts are good and not evil. I want to remind you that God is up to something good, and He has you in mind—above and beyond what you could ask or imagine!

Father, awaken me to the many ways You are speaking to me. I don't want to miss anything You have to say. You are up to something good. You have plans for me that are exceedingly abundantly above anything I could ask You for or think of. I could never outdo You. No matter how lofty my desires and goals, Your thoughts and Your ways will always be higher than mine. Thank You for having such a good plan for me. Cause my will to work in perfect harmony with Yours. In Jesus's name, amen.

February 7

How Are You Building Your Life?

Therefore whoever hears these sayings of Mine, and does them, I will liken him to a wise man who built his house on the rock: and the rain descended, the floods came, and the winds blew and beat on that house; and it did not fall, for it was founded on the rock.
—Matthew 7:24–25

Our lives are built by a series of thoughts, much as bricks are used to build a house. The bricks are what bring it forth from a piece of paper and make it three-dimensional. As a man thinks in his heart—in the present active continuum—he is building his life one brick at a time. Your every present thought is a significant building block in determining the quality of your future. Many of us build lives like shanties, while others build mansions. If your thoughts are inferior, your life will be inferior; but if your thoughts are lofty and honorable, you are laying the foundation to live accordingly.

Father, I choose to honor You with my thoughts. I resist negative, self-defeating mind-sets and choose instead to speak life and strength into my day. I decree and declare that I am blessed. All my physical needs are met, and I have more than enough to give to others. I work diligently and with a spirit of excellence. I declare that my home and workspace are peaceful. I maximize my potential and move boldly toward my destiny. In Jesus's name, amen.

February 8

Quality Matters

For whatever is in your heart determines what you say. A good person produces good things from the treasury of a good heart, and an evil person produces evil things from the treasury of an evil heart.
—Matthew 12:34–35, NLT

There is a direct correlation between the quality of your thoughts and the quality of your life. What you think determines who you are; it determines what you are, where you go, what you acquire, where you live, whom you love, where you work, what you accomplish, what you read—I could go on and on. James Allen wrote in his timeless classic *As a Man Thinketh*, "All that a man achieves and all that he fails to achieve is the direct result of his own thoughts."[2] If your life is going to change, you must think for a change. You are always only one thought away from changing your life.

Lord, I know that as I think in my heart, so am I. Upgrade my thoughts and give me a kingdom paradigm. I put negative, self-defeating thoughts under my feet. They have no place in my life. Father, cause my speech to reflect Your will, and usher me into new emotional, intellectual, professional, spiritual, and financial territory. I put no limits on what You can and will do through me. In Jesus's name, amen.

February 9

Your Thoughts Create Your Reality

The backslider in heart [from God and from fearing God] shall be filled with [the fruit of] his own ways, and a good man shall be satisfied with [the fruit of] his ways [with the holy thoughts and actions which his heart prompts and in which he delights].

—Proverbs 14:14, AMP

Here's the principle: You will never have more or go farther or accomplish greater things than your thoughts will allow you. Therefore, you must create an opulent thinking environment in order to create an opulent life. Your life is a reflection of your most dominant thoughts and meditations. When you make it a practice to meditate on success, you will begin to live a successful life.

I decree and declare that I am living my most blessed and best days now. I am crowned with God's love and mercy. With all good things He satisfies me. I do my work as unto the Lord with diligence and a spirit of excellence. I work according to God's daily agenda and perform for an audience of one—the Lord Jesus Christ. The Lord is teaching me how to improve my productivity—to work smarter and more efficiently; He gives me an outstanding attitude and I produce superior work. Thank You, Father, for ordering my steps according to Your original plan and purpose for me. In Jesus's name, amen.

February 10

Be Specific About It

So Solomon built the temple and finished it. And he built the inside walls of the temple with cedar boards; from the floor of the temple to the ceiling he paneled the inside with wood; and he covered the floor of the temple with planks of cypress.... And in the eleventh year, in the month of Bul, which is the eighth month, the house was finished in all its details and according to all its plans.

—1 Kings 6:14–38

It is not enough just to meditate on success generally; you need to be specific. You are the architect and building contractor of your future. Use your thoughts as an architect uses a blueprint. Think about every detail. An architect not only thinks about the rooms in a house but also the types of windows, the size of closets, the location of outlets, and so on. Nothing is too insignificant. Think big and think detailed!

Father, I believe You have designed me to be a success and to prosper physically, financially, relationally, socially, spiritually, and in every other way a person can prosper. I declare that I have an excellent spirit and do not procrastinate. I work as unto the Lord. I am an influencer, and I leave a legacy for the next generation. My environment is prosperous and healthy. In the name of Jesus I declare that I will live authentically and accomplish that which I was born to do. In the name of Jesus, amen.

February 11

What Do You Want to See Happen?

Jabez called on the God of Israel saying, "Oh, that You would bless me indeed, and enlarge my territory, that Your hand would be with me, and that You would keep me from evil, that I may not cause pain!" So God granted him what he requested.
—1 Chronicles 4:10

If you want your life to be different, you must dare to think differently—dare to think outside of the box. Think possibility thoughts. It could be for this very reason that Jabez did not ask God for more property or greater wealth but to enlarge his intellectual territory—or his mental capacity regarding his own worth. He asked God to give him a greater capacity for conceiving what he might accomplish on God's behalf because he knew his own limited thinking was holding him captive. He prayed that God would give him a greater ability to think big. You need to cultivate possibility thinking because your thoughts determine your destiny.

Father, I will not see myself as inferior. Like Jabez, I boldly ask You to enlarge my territory. Let every region You have purposed for me be released in Your perfect timing. Thank You, Father, for working everything together to advance Your will for my life. In Jesus's name, amen.

February 12

Go Beyond Borders

For I will cast out the nations before you and enlarge your borders.
—Exodus 34:24

Nothing limits achievement like small thinking—nothing expands possibilities like thinking outside of the box. Unleash the power of your mind. Learn to cultivate possibility thinking. Think original thoughts. In 1886 John Pemberton turned common medicinal syrup into a cultural phenomenon by combining it with carbonated water and serving it as a refreshing drink. Coca-Cola is now the most widely known beverage on the planet. Think about something that has never been done, or put a new spin on something that has always been around.

Father, because You know no limits, I will not put myself in a box. I am made in Your image, after Your likeness. You put creativity in my DNA. You are a revealer of secrets. Download into my mind prophetic strategies and cutting-edge tactics that can propel me to the next level in my profession, finances, family, and/or ministry. Lord, sharpen my spiritual ears so I can hear clearly as You share Your divine insights. In Jesus's name, amen.

February 13

SEE WITH NEW EYES

If people can't see what God is doing, they stumble all over themselves; but when they attend to what he reveals, they are most blessed.
—PROVERBS 29:18, THE MESSAGE

Determine now what steps you need to take on a daily basis to make the most of your life in the future. I like what Henry David Thoreau says: "Go confidently in the direction of your dreams. Live the life you have imagined."[3] Sometimes you need to see with new eyes. The possibilities in your life change when your perspective changes. This is true vision.

Father, give me true vision to see the possibilities You see. Cause my spiritual eyes to function with 20/20 vision for the correct insight, understanding, and interpretations of Your movements. Cause fresh winds of the Holy Spirit to blow. Open my eyes so I can see my circumstances, abilities, and potential in new light. In Jesus's name I pray, amen.

February 14

What Is Your Vision?

That night the answer to the mystery was given to Daniel in a vision. Daniel blessed the God of heaven, saying, "Blessed be the name of God, forever and ever. He knows all, does all: He changes the seasons and guides history, He raises up kings and also brings them down, He provides both intelligence and discernment, He opens up the depths, tells secrets, sees in the dark—light spills out of him!"

—Daniel 2:19–22, The Message

Vision connects you to your destiny and future. Helen Keller said, "The greatest tragedy in life is people who have sight but no vision."[4] You must see yourself doing more, gaining more, and being more. Vision is the ability to think progressively. A vision is a mental image of future possibilities.

In the name of Jesus I confess today that I only progress. I will persist until I succeed. I walk in dominion and authority. There is no slackness in my hand. Where I stand, God gives me the land. The blessings of the Lord make me rich, and I am daily loaded with benefits. I call forth every individual and resource assigned to assist me in fulfilling my kingdom assignment during this season. I declare that I attract only the things, people, and resources suitable to undergird and facilitate God's plan and purpose for my life. In Jesus's name, amen.

February 15

Chart Unknown Territories

If the Lord your God enlarges your territory, as He has sworn to your fathers to do, and gives you all the land which He promised to your fathers to give, if you keep all these commandments to do them, which I command you this day, to love the Lord your God and to walk always in His ways, then you shall add three other cities to these three.
—Deuteronomy 19:8–9, amp

A friend of mine once told me that your feet will never take you where your mind has never been. Become the Christopher Columbus of your future. Columbus dared to lose sight of the known in order to experience the unknown. To conquer new territories you must have courage to lose sight of the shore. Dream big, then dare to wake up and accomplish it. Motivational speaker Robert J. Kriegel has said, "The shame in life is not to fail to reach your dream, but to fail to have a dream to reach."

I declare in the name of Jesus that I am a pioneer of new territories. I walk in favor with God and man, and I will possess all the land God has given me. There will be no holdups, no holdouts, no setbacks or delays. I will not look back to return to the old. Father, cause me to ascend into new realms of power and authority and access new dimensions of divine revelation. Breathe new life into every dormant dream. In the name of Jesus, amen.

February 16

Think Progress

As for you, O king, thoughts came to your mind while on your bed, about what would come to pass after this; and He who reveals secrets has made known to you what will be.

—Daniel 2:29

If you want to progress in life, you have to think progressive thoughts. To do so, something new must replace the old. You have to think beyond where you are. Alexander Graham Bell thought beyond the limitation of the dots and dashes of the Morse code and replaced the telegraph with the innovation of the telephone. Become a visionary—be creative. Take the limits off your mind!

I take the limits off my mind! You desire to fill my mind with the creativity that flows forth from Your Spirit. So I open my mind and heart to receive fresh vision, new revelation, and divine insight from You. Even at night I expect to receive innovative strategy and witty ideas through visions and dreams. From this day forward I align my speech with where I'm going, not with where I am. I confess that I am progressing toward my destiny and not regressing. I speak life into every dead dream and awaken the hope for the future. Father, I will attain all You have for me. In Jesus's name, amen.

February 17

Shut Down the Enemy

In that coming day no weapon turned against you will succeed. You will silence every voice raised up to accuse you.
—Isaiah 54:17, NLT

You must lift your voice and come in fury and passion to put to shame all the contrivances of the enemy. You must act offensively. You cannot let the plans Satan has for the children of God come to pass. Not today. Not on your watch. Not ever! Every attack leveled against your loved ones opens up the opportunity to plunder the enemies' possessions and territory instead of the other way around. You may not have chosen Satan as an enemy, but he has chosen you. Yet God has given you the power to shut down every initiative instituted by anyone and everyone who moves by satanic impulse. Their provocations to attack you will serve you instead.

Father, place a warrior's anointing upon me. Cause every domain and system that You have assigned me to be released in the name of Jesus. Strengthen the hedge of protection around my life, my possessions, my family, my friends and associates, and my ministry. I declare that I am more than a conqueror! Destiny-altering activities must cease. I will possess the land You have given me. In the name of Jesus, amen.

Train Your Spiritual Senses

Son of man, I have made you a watchman for the house of Israel; therefore hear a word from My mouth, and give them warning from Me.
—Ezekiel 3:17

The Bible is replete with scriptures and stories supporting the relevance of watching and praying, and it is no less significant to modern-day believers interested in hearing from God and aligning with His will. They are vigilant not to judge by what they see with their natural eyes or hear with their natural ears. Instead, they allow the Holy Spirit to train their spiritual senses so they become sharp and accurate concerning spiritual matters.

Father, I do not put my confidence in what I see. I put my confidence in You and Your Word. I am who You say I am, and I can accomplish what You say I can accomplish. Almighty God, sharpen my spiritual discernment that I may hear You clearly. Let prophetic insight be upon me today. Place upon me Issachar's anointing for the discernment of correct times and seasons. Give me wisdom and direction. "Cause me to know the way in which I should walk, for I lift up my soul to You" (Ps. 143:8). Dismantle evil powers working to frustrate my day, assignments, and activities. In Jesus's name, amen.

February 19

Get the Divine Download

I tell you the truth, the Son can do nothing by himself; he can do only what he sees his Father doing, because whatever the Father does the Son also does. For the Father loves the Son and shows him all he does. Yes, to your amazement he will show him even greater things than these.

—John 5:19–20, NIV

Follow the example of Jesus. Jesus said that when other people were unable to see what was going on in heaven, He could. This is the challenge of creative thinking—as you open the spiritual channels of your mind, God can download divine, creative thoughts into your brain. Ask God to enlarge your capacity for thinking, to take the limits off.

Father, I reaffirm my commitment to take the limits off of You. Allow me to tap into Your creative mind—Your genius—and see what other people cannot see and hear what other people cannot hear. As You release divine downloads, I will not doubt the plans and strategies You reveal. I will not fear unchartered territory. Father, place upon me Moses's anointing as a trailblazer and leader. Enlarge the capacity of my mind so that I think big and not small. Let Your kingdom come and Your will be done on earth as it is in heaven. In Jesus's name, amen.

February 20

Can You Hear the Beat?

This vision is for a future time. It describes the end, and it will be fulfilled. If it seems slow in coming, wait patiently, for it will surely take place. It will not be delayed.
—Habakkuk 2:3, NLT

God will not only grant you your prayerful requests, but He will also grant you your daily declarations. Just as Jabez altered his destiny by asking God to give him bigger thoughts, you can change yours too. I challenge you to change your role from being a cheerleader to becoming a drum major. March to the beat of your own drum, to the rhythm of your individuality, and to the symphonic pulsating sounds of your unique destiny and purpose.

Father, I praise You for I am fearfully and wonderfully made. You used Your divine skill to put me together, and I am perfectly suited for my unique assignment in the earth. I have been divinely fitted with creativity and ingenuity. I am a problem solver, and I am becoming an expert in my field. I have favor with You and man. I am able to meet any obstacle I face today. You have done all things well, and that includes making me. I expect You to do great and mighty things in and through me. In Jesus's name, amen.

February 21

Focus on the Positive

Summing it all up, friends, I'd say you'll do best by filling your minds and meditating on things true, noble, reputable, authentic, compelling, gracious—the best, not the worst; the beautiful, not the ugly; things to praise, not things to curse.

—Philippians 4:8, The Message

Whatever your predominant focus is, that is what you permit to exist in your life. Jabez chose to focus on his future desires rather than his present circumstances. Many times people focus on the negative, and they live in a cycle of negativity. You have to choose to focus on the positive. You have to train your mind to think on whatever is honest, virtuous, and praiseworthy. Whatever is going wrong in your life is a result of your focus. If you don't like it, change your focus!

Father, bring my thoughts into divine alignment today. I choose to think about things that are true, noble, reputable, authentic, compelling, and gracious. I meditate on the best, not the worst; the beautiful, not the ugly. You are my earnest expectation and my hope. Because of You, I know I can experience exceedingly abundantly above all that I could ask or think. Because of You, I know I am victorious. I declare that new cycles of victory, success, and prosperity will replace old cycles of failure, poverty, and death. In Jesus's name, amen.

February 22

Visualize the Expanse

And the Lord said to Abram…"Lift your eyes now and look from the place where you are—northward, southward, eastward, and westward; for all the land which you see I give to you and your descendants forever.…Arise, walk in the land through its length and its width, for I give it to you."
—Genesis 13:14–17

God taught Abraham something about focus. He told him to look at the territory He was giving him, walk the land in every direction, and visualize the expanse of his legacy. Then He said to him, "I will make your descendants as the dust of the earth; so that if a man could number the dust of the earth, then your descendants also could be numbered" (Gen. 13:16). What did God train Abraham to do? He trained him to focus on bigger thoughts. If you plan to change your future, do not focus on things or people smaller than what you are hoping for. Your focus will either feed your faith or confirm your fears. Learn to think like Abraham. Think intentionally, generationally, and even globally. You can never think too big, too grand, or too great!

I choose to think big and expect great things for my future. I decree open doors and divine connections. I am taking the limits off You, and I declare that I will walk in the fullness of all You have for me. In the name of Jesus, amen.

February 23

What's Surrounding You?

When He had come out of the boat, immediately there met Him out of the tombs a man with an unclean spirit....And always, night and day, he was in the mountains and in the tombs, crying out and cutting himself with stones.
—Mark 5:2–5

Your environment will impact your attitude, focus, faith, and the intentionality of your thoughts. If you are surrounded by clutter, noise, reminders of lack, and other problems, you will find it more difficult to think past those limiting issues—just as the man in the tombs could not move past the barrenness of his environment.

I like beauty—anything that's beautiful, clean, and orderly automatically gives me inspiration. Some people like the quiet of nature or the stimulation of music or a bustling café. God gave man a myriad of inspirational environments to spur his creativity. You have the power to create an inspirational environment around yourself. Look for those particular environments that inspire thoughts of abundance on every level, and find a way to spend blocks of time in your most creative space.

Father, spark my creativity. Let me find a space where I can enjoy Your beauty and find inspiration. Bring order to my environment. Let my home and every place I frequent be filled with Your peace. In the name of Jesus, amen.

Pretend You're Already There

Just then a woman who had hemorrhaged for twelve years slipped in from behind and lightly touched his robe. She was thinking to herself, "If I can just put a finger on his robe, I'll get well." Jesus turned—caught her at it. Then he reassured her: "Courage, daughter. You took a risk of faith, and now you're well." The woman was well from then on.

—Matthew 9:20–22, The Message

The biggest risk in life is not taking any risk at all! Prepare your mind to seek after and accept greater challenges. If you have trouble thinking outside of the box, then imagine creating a new one. Become comfortable with thoughts of achievement and success—think and feel as if you already have what you desire. Create the feelings of success by pretending you are living the kind of life you have imagined until this practice affects the habits of your mind. Think in the present, and think positively—see the thing you desire as if you already have it. Condition your mind to accept these thoughts, and you will draw these opportunities and experiences to yourself.

If I continue to do what I've been doing, I will reap the same results. So I choose to expand the borders of my thoughts. I see myself blessed and walking in divine favor, fully equipped with all I need to complete my kingdom assignment. I greet each day with expectation because You are leading me by Your hand. Amen.

February 25

God Wants Your Abundance

For I know the thoughts that I think toward you, says the Lord, *thoughts of peace and not of evil, to give you a future and a hope.*
—Jeremiah 29:11

The first thing you need to change is your thoughts about what God wants for you. He wants you to live a life of abundance. It is His desire to give you divine universal secrets to great success and prosperity. He holds the secret spiritual recipe for abundant living.

There are many people who may not be as spiritual as you are, but nevertheless they were able to tap into something great. Whether by accident or providence, they are living lives beyond their wildest dreams, and you can too. You must say to yourself, until this one fact becomes your conviction, "God wants me to live in abundance!" A world of possibilities is waiting to be released in your future.

You want me to live in abundance! I decree and declare that I am prosperous in every way a person can prosper: spiritually, physically, financially, relationally, intellectually, emotionally, and so on. My thoughts must align with Your desires for me. I reject every self-defeating thought and put it under my feet. I declare that I am blessed with all spiritual blessings in heavenly places in the name of Jesus, amen!

Look Through Eyes of Blessing

Now [David] was ruddy, with bright eyes, and good-looking. And the Lord said, "Arise, anoint him; for this is the one!" Then Samuel took the horn of oil and anointed him in the midst of his brothers; and the Spirit of the Lord came upon David from that day forward.

—1 Samuel 16:12–13

Samuel went to David and poured anointing oil over his head to signify he would be the next king of Israel. It was many years later before David actually wore his crown, but from the moment he was anointed, he was already a king in God's eyes. Good things began to happen to him almost immediately because he started looking at his world through eyes of blessing rather than eyes of failure. Even as he overcame the lion and the bear, he knew he could overcome giants. And just as he took authority and overcame everything that threatened his ascent to the throne, you must take authority and overcome everything that threatens your ascent into the realm of success and prosperity.

I decree and declare that I am anointed for my assignment. No weapon formed against me shall prosper. Though I have not reached my promised land, I decree that I will walk in the fullness of all God has promised because His Word will not return void. In the name of Jesus, amen.

February 27

Decree Your Future

You are a chosen generation, a royal priesthood, a holy nation, His own special people, that you may proclaim the praises of Him who called you out of darkness into His marvelous light.
—1 Peter 2:9

A king does not beg and cry for anything. He doesn't have to. He declares something, and that thing is established. A king has the legal power to *decree,* which is an old English word for *legislate.* He institutes, he confirms, he settles, he summons, he authorizes—that's what a king does. Peter tells us we belong to "a royal priesthood." The word *royal* speaks of our kingly attributes as believers. Remember, Jesus is King of kings—He is the capital *K* King, and we are the lowercase *k* kings. You must manifest your royal anointing to decree blessings over your marriage, family, business, ministry, and every other realm of your life.

I declare Your Word over my life today. I am blessed exceedingly, abundantly above any level I could imagine. According to Deuteronomy 28, I am blessed in the city and in the field; I am blessed when I come and when I go. I am fruitful and lack no good thing. I am blessed socially, financially, spiritually, emotionally, and intellectually. My family is blessed; my workplace is blessed; my church is blessed. Because of You, I eat the good of the land. Thank You, Lord! Amen.

Give the Universe What It Wants

For the earnest expectation of the creation eagerly waits for the revealing of the sons of God.
—Romans 8:19

The whole universe is waiting for us to give it instruction. The whole universe waits in anticipation for the sons and daughters of God to manifest themselves and bring it back into alignment with God's original intent for them. Every word you speak is pregnant with regal, creative power.

The first to illustrate this was God Himself. According to Hebrews 11:3, "The universe was created by the word of God, so that *what is seen was not made out of things that are visible*" (ESV, emphasis added). Words are the "things" that this verse is referring to. Even though words are not visible, they are substantive entities that brought tangibility to the universe through the power of God.

You brought the world into existence with Your words, and You have put life and death in the power of my tongue. I stand in the authority You have given me, and I decree that every element of my day will cooperate with Your plans and purposes. I will do nothing of my own but only as You lead. Cause my will to work in perfect harmony with Yours. In Jesus's name, amen.

February 29

Get Connected to God

And when you are praying, do not use meaningless repetition as the Gentiles do, for they suppose that they will be heard for their many words. So do not be like them; for your Father knows what you need before you ask Him.

—Matthew 6:7–8, nas

Prayer is not some kind of mechanical practice that will get the same response to the same words each time like a magical incantation. Prayer is not sorcery or witchcraft. Prayer is about connecting with God and getting His word on whatever we are facing, and then acting accordingly. Often Jesus *became* the answer after He had prayed. There seems to always have been a corresponding action.

Father, give me prophetic downloads so that my words will be more than motivation. Let them be life. Let Your Word renew my mind and make me more like You. This is a new season, and You are aligning me with Your original plan and purpose. Let me be perfectly in sync and in season with You. Father, as I press in to hear You, give me a word for each situation I face today. Your kingdom is my priority and Your assignment is my pleasure. Let Your kingdom come and Your will be done on the earth as it is in heaven. In the name of Jesus, amen.

March

March 1

Words Are a Spiritual Mystery

You will also declare a thing, and it will be established for you; so light will shine on your ways.
—Job 22:28

Scripture is replete with principles that support the power of the tongue. This verse refers to your royal anointing—the favor God has poured over you because you belong to Him. The true power of the spoken word is beyond our common understanding. It is a spiritual mystery—a hidden secret now being revealed to equip God's people for an unprecedented era of empowerment and influence. The time has come for believers to rise up and walk in the knowledge and authority God has provided and commanded through His Word—the Word He spoke into us and created us to speak forth. While forces around us threaten our peace and stability, nothing can prevail against God's spoken Word.

I decree and declare that my spirit man is clad with the armor of the Lord. Evil shall not come near my dwelling because I dwell in the secret place of the Most High God and abide under the shadow of the Almighty. I declare that I am victorious in You, and every mountain that is preventing me from possessing my inheritance in You must move now in the name of Jesus, amen.

What's Your Combination?

Death and life are in the power of the tongue,
and those who love it will eat its fruit.
—Proverbs 18:21

Consciously choosing your words is like putting together the right combination of bricks and mortar. Just as the great architects have taken raw materials to build skyscrapers and timeless monuments, your words are the raw materials that can form the life you are meant to live. Words carry great power. It is the word of God that comes forth from your mouth that pulls all the resources of heaven into your situation. (See Matthew 18:18.)

I build my future with the words I speak today. Therefore I align my speech with the Word of God because God's Word is His will for me. I am not here by accident. I was made for this time and this season, and everything I need to fulfill God's purposes for me today is already in my hand. I decree and declare that my mission today shall be unobstructed. Father, empower me to serve You in holiness and righteousness. In the name of Jesus, amen.

March 3

Take Care How You Steer

Look also at ships: although they are so large and are driven by fierce winds, they are turned by a very small rudder wherever the pilot desires. Even so the tongue is a little member that boasts great things.

—James 3:4–5

When a ship sets sail to cross the sea, the pilot plots out the course. Then he determines the times he will need to adjust the direction of the ship to follow the course he has set. For the pilot, the course is created first in his thoughts, communicated through the rudder, and then realized as the rest of the ship lines up with his intent. For us, our lives arrive at our desired goals only if we line up our thoughts, words, habits, and actions in a similar way. Rather than letting the elements of your day dictate your destiny, you can take control of these elements and direct their course to a greater end.

I decree and declare that I do not just let life happen to me. I seek Your desires for me, and my words and actions align with those plans. I will not allow challenges to alter my focus. I will remain steadfast until I reach my "expected end" (Jer. 29:11, KJV). In Jesus's name, amen.

Daydream About Possibilities

*The Lord will work out his plans for my life—
for your faithful love, O Lord, endures forever. Don't abandon me, for you made me.*
—Psalm 138:8, NLT

You must take the time to consider carefully the course of your life. Where are you heading? What will it look like when you get there?

Let your imagination take over. Spend time daydreaming about where you want to be in life. Read about it. Study that place. Write about it in your journal. Draw it. Paint it. Let your mind run free with the possibilities of what you can attain, what you can be, and what you can accomplish. Transform your imaginations into intentions. Act intentionally rather than react unconsciously.

Now talk about it. Line up your mouth—the rudder of your life—with where you are going. Then keep it steady and on course.

Nothing is impossible with God; therefore I will not limit what He can do through me. I free my mind and heart to dream. I call forth those dreams the Holy Spirit placed in my heart long ago, dreams I buried because of fear or unbelief. I command them to wake up. Father, my heart is open to receive Your desires for me. I only want to do Your will. Amen.

March 5

Don't Double Back

He who doubts is like a wave of the sea driven and tossed by the wind. For let not that man suppose that he will receive anything from the Lord; he is a double-minded man, unstable in all his ways.

—James 1:6–8

What happens to a ship if you head it in one direction at one moment, and then turn it in the opposite direction in the next—and keep doing that over and over? Pretty simple—it goes nowhere. This is what happens when people start speaking about the good things they are expecting to happen one minute and then spend the next half hour talking about all the negative things happening to them that are keeping them from getting there. They are turning their lives in circles. They line up their spoken words with where they want to go for a little while; then when they meet a storm along the way, all they do is talk about the bad weather and lose track of where they were headed in the first place. They forget they have the power to turn their lives around in the storm or press on through it to the sunshine on the other side. They forget that the "Son" has never stopped shining on their lives, no matter how dark the clouds in the sky are.

Father, help me to keep my focus on You in the face of my trials. You are greater than every challenge I face. Let my words always reflect that truth. Amen.

Decree What Will Happen

I will declare the decree: the Lord has said to Me, "You are My Son, today I have begotten You. Ask of Me, and I will give You the nations for your inheritance and the ends of the earth for Your possession."
—Psalm 2:7–8

Your every decree is pregnant with the power and potential to revolutionize your life. David used his right to decree and declare to turn the tides of Israel's unfavorable fate and to defeat their enemy Goliath. Since the spirit realm is the causal realm, Goliath was dead long before he was struck by the stone and beheaded by the sword.

I realize the supernatural realm is where victories are won. So I declare the victory in Jesus's name. I declare victory over every Goliath in my life—in my family, my finances, my workplace, my church/ministry, and my body. I decree and declare that today is the dawning of a new season of success and fruitfulness. Old things have passed away; behold, all things are becoming new. In Jesus's name, amen.

March 7

Bless All Things

Bless those who persecute you; bless and do not curse.
—Romans 12:14

Choose to use your tongue to bring life and not death, to bless and not to curse—even when it comes to your enemies. Learn the art of blessing, for in blessing a thing or a person, that thing or person must bless you. When you bless, blessings will be drawn to you, or as Deuteronomy 28:2 says, "Blessings shall come upon you and overtake you." Conversely, in cursing a thing or a person, you draw curses upon yourself.

Let my speech be always with grace that it may minister to the hearer. I want to be blessed, so I bless others and do not curse them. I choose to forgive and not condemn. I judge nothing and no one prematurely. I decree and declare that a guard is set over my mouth. I keep a tight rein on my tongue and honor You with my words. In the name of Jesus, amen.

Attend to Your Words

He who guards his mouth [watches what he says] preserves his life.
—Proverbs 13:3

I am convinced that, because of ignorance, believers tend to live beneath the standard God has ordained for His children. We do not know that our daily declarations and decrees have the power to alter our destinies and change the quality of our lives. As James said, "If anyone does not stumble in word, he is a perfect [mature] man, able also to bridle the whole body" (James 3:2). If guarding your words causes you to keep your life and grow in maturity, imagine what happens when you do not guard your words.

I want Your best, so I speak life and not death. I position myself to receive from You by honoring You both with my words and deeds. My tongue has the power to determine what direction I go, so I choose my words wisely. I fill my mouth with praise, and I speak forth Your Word. Because Your Word is a lamp unto my feet, I do not stumble or fall. My steps are secure. I am crowned with Your love and mercy. With good things You satisfy me all the days of my life. In Jesus's name, amen.

March 9

Don't Scoff at a Blessing

Then Elisha said, "Hear the word of the Lord. Thus says the Lord: 'Tomorrow about this time a seah of fine flour shall be sold for a shekel, and two seahs of barley for a shekel, at the gate of Samaria.'"

So an officer on whose hand the king leaned answered the man of God and said, "Look, if the Lord would make windows in heaven, could this thing be?" And he said, "In fact, you shall see it with your eyes, but you shall not eat of it."

—2 Kings 7:1–2

The prophet Elisha spoke the blessing of God into manifestation. It took one prophetic declaration to change the economic landscape of an entire nation. The officer who influenced the king met divine declaration with skepticism and unbelief. His words literally aborted the blessing of God for him and caused him instead to lose his life. This man died because he refused to agree with the plan of God and scoffed at the methodology of a blessing. Take care that you do not do the same.

Lord, I will not scoff at Your ways. I will cooperate with Your plans and purposes for me. Even when I don't understand what You're doing or why, I trust You. I will not laugh as Sarah did. I will not doubt as Thomas did. I will not operate in my own strength. I humble myself before You and follow You, Lord. You have my total trust. Amen.

Speak What Is True

Do not be deceived, God is not mocked; for whatever a man sows, that he will also reap. For he who sows to his flesh will of the flesh reap corruption, but he who sows to the Spirit will of the Spirit reap everlasting life.
—Galatians 6:7–8

Place your hand directly in front of your mouth and declare aloud, "I am blessed, all of my needs are met, and I have more than enough for myself, my household, and extra left over to give to others." Did you feel the power of those words coming forth out of your mouth like a breeze? Your words will come back to you, manifested with hurricane force, blowing into your life abundance and blessings or lack and calamity depending on what you spoke out. Choose to steer your life into blessings by filling the atmosphere around you with words of faith and victory.

I release my name into the atmosphere and declare that I have a good reputation. My name is associated with excellence, integrity, holiness, generosity, vision, health, and faith. I am anointed for such a time as this to walk fully in my purpose. Father, according to Isaiah 54:17, no weapon formed against me shall prosper, and every tongue that rises against me in judgment You shall condemn. This is my heritage as a servant of the Lord. Through You I am empowered to see victory. In Jesus's name, amen.

March 11

Words Have Power and Presence

Do you see a man who is hasty in his words?
There is more hope for a fool than for him.
—Proverbs 29:20, esv

Words released into the atmosphere do not disappear and dissipate. They have no geographical limitations. Words have power, presence, and prophetic implications. They create a magnetic force that pulls the manifestation of what you speak—good or bad, blessing or cursing—from other realms, regions, and dimensions. They are suspended and incubated in the realm of the spirit awaiting the correct time and optimum condition for manifestation.

I commit to attaining and maintaining a positive mind-set. I will study Your Word and declare Your truth on a daily basis. Let the wisdom from Your Word influence my thoughts until my life and speech reflect Your Word. I thank You for rock-solid faith that does not doubt Your Word. I know I am not here by accident. You have placed me here to fulfill Your purpose. You have called me to be a leader within my sphere of influence, and I commit to bear Your light as a change agent in a dark world. Today is the beginning of a new season of increase and productivity. In the name of Jesus, amen.

Your Mouth Legislates

But Joshua the son of Nun and Caleb the son of Jephunneh...spoke to all the congregation of the children of Israel, saying: "The land we passed through to spy out is an exceedingly good land. If the Lord delights in us, then He will bring us into this land and give it to us, 'a land which flows with milk and honey.' Only do not rebel against the Lord, nor fear the people of the land, for they are our bread; their protection has departed from them, and the Lord is with us. Do not fear them." And all the congregation said to stone them with stones.

—Numbers 14:6–10

The children of Israel wandered in the wilderness for forty years and died, not because they were lost but because they legislated their wandering exile with their own mouths. Because of their capricious, negative, and ungrateful chatter, they ignorantly altered their destiny from a journey that should have lasted approximately a fortnight to one of forty years. Was this fate of the devil, the original plan of God, or their own doing? Scripture clearly reveals that the forty-year wilderness journey occurred as a result of their own ensnaring words.

Father, I decree and declare that this year is pregnant with purpose. The best is yet to come. The pain of my yesterday will not appear in my tomorrow. Father, give me strategies for fruitfulness and let my life reflect Your glory. In Jesus's name, amen.

March 13

Live on Purpose

See then that you walk circumspectly, not as fools but as wise, redeeming the time, because the days are evil.
—Ephesians 5:15–16

One of the wisest things we can do is to live life on purpose. We are to be intentional with how we order our days and spend our time. Everyone in the universe has been given the same quantity of time—we all get twenty-four hours per day whether we live in the White House or the ghetto. What we do with those twenty-four hours determines what we accomplish in our lifetime.

Father, I decree and declare that I am empowered to accomplish everything I was born to do. My destiny and my speech are in sync with Your will. I am an influencer. I leave a legacy for future generations. I walk in peace with You and mankind. You prosper the works of my hands. My family, life, and friends are abundantly blessed. Because of You, I have the courage to remain true to my convictions as I live out my assignment in the earth. In Jesus's name, amen.

What Will You Choose to Believe?

As soon as we heard these things, our hearts melted; neither did there remain any more courage in anyone because of you, for the Lord your God, He is God in heaven above and on earth beneath.
—Joshua 2:11

While the Israelites were calling those in Canaan "giants," the hearts of those "giants" were melting in fear of the Israelites. Instead of listening to Joshua and Caleb, whose words filled the atmosphere with faith, they chose instead to suck all hope from their surroundings by listening instead to the other ten spies who spoke only of their inability and the greatness of their enemies. They even tried to repent when they realized what they had done and decided to try to obey God in taking the land, but it was too late—their own words had already undone them.

Father, thank You for giving me absolute assurance that You are in control. I greet obstacles with rock-solid faith. I arise today knowing that You hear and answer prayer. Father, release divine angelic escorts to safely lead me into goodly places. The light of Your Word illuminates my path. By its principles I blaze new trails and defy the status quo. I discover new horizons within my chosen field. I walk in step with You. I remain in perfect peace because I put my trust in You and not in man. In Jesus's name, amen.

March 15

Fill the Atmosphere With Victory

Just as you have spoken in My hearing, so I will do to you: The carcasses of you who have complained against Me shall fall in this wilderness, all of you who were numbered, according to your entire number, from twenty years old and above. Except for Caleb the son of Jephunneh and Joshua the son of Nun, you shall by no means enter the land which I swore I would make you dwell in.

—Numbers 14:28–30

Even though Israel acted on God's word to them, they filled the atmosphere with their fear and defeat rather than faith and victory. What they received was not according to God's promises but according to what they filled the atmosphere with. They steered their lives into a port of fear and failure, dropped anchor there—and then they were surprised that the water was filled with nothing but sharks. They snatched defeat right out of the mouth of victory. Just like these Israelites, are you getting exactly what you have always been asking for?

Father, I arise today in Your strength, determined to use the gifts You have given me to be a blessing to my family, community, and nation. I declare that I am more than a conqueror. I will forever be first and not last, above and not beneath. Guard me today against both pride and false humility, and let my speech only create a pathway to victory. In Jesus's name, amen.

What Do You Believe?

But the Lord was angry with me [Moses] on your account, and would not listen to me. So the Lord said to me, "Enough of that! Speak no more to Me of this matter. Go up to the top of Pisgah, and lift your eyes toward the west, the north, the south, and the east; behold it with your eyes, for you shall not cross over this Jordan."
—Deuteronomy 3:26–27

When you read one of God's promises to you in the Bible, what is your first thought? Do you think, "Oh, it will be wonderful to have that someday in heaven," or "What a wonderful promise! Of course, that is not for someone as miserable as me." Or do you think, "Praise God! If He says that I should have that, then nothing can stop His blessing from manifesting in my life!" Unfortunately, too many pick the first two. Just as the Israelites did standing on the bank of the Jordan looking at what was promised them, we too often choose to give up before the battle even begins.

Father, I pursue the purpose You have for me with courage and conviction. I believe Your Word and count what You say as done. I receive all of Your promises as yes in You and amen. You are with me always, and I know I will never be put to shame. In Jesus's name, amen.

March 17

Take God at His Word

Then one of them, a lawyer, asked Him a question, testing Him, saying, "Teacher, which is the greatest commandment in the law?"
—Matthew 22:35–36

Now, we tend to make fun of lawyers and politicians in our culture today, but throughout history lawyers have revealed some of the greatest things about God we have ever known. Moses was "the lawgiver," and the apostle Paul was a Pharisee. Martin Luther of the Reformation began his career by entering law school, as did the great revivalist Charles Finney. What made them so powerful? They read their Bibles as lawyers would when studying to prepare a case, and they put more faith in God keeping His Word than they did in any earthly laws. Then they took those words and charged the atmosphere around them with biblical truth. They changed their worlds through what they spoke.

I take You at Your Word. Because of what Jesus did on the cross, I know I am a son of God and that I am seated in heavenly places in Christ. You withhold no good thing from those who walk uprightly, so I commit my ways to You. Father, I ask that You lead me along paths of righteousness and cause my latter days to be greater than my former. In Jesus's name, amen.

March 18

God's Promises Are for You

Thus says the Lord God to these bones: "Surely I will cause breath to enter into you, and you shall live. I will put sinews on you and bring flesh upon you, cover you with skin and put breath in you; and you shall live. Then you shall know that I am the Lord."

—Ezekiel 37:5

When you read the Bible, you need to take God's Word personally. His promises are for His people, and if you have given your life to Him as your Lord and Savior, then that means *you*. Speak life into your dead areas—you'll be amazed at what God's words in your mouth will do for you. If God has said it, then that should settle it for us.

Through You I can do all things. Let me be more aware of Your presence and power in my life today. I will proclaim Your Word. I decree and declare that my environment is prosperous, my family is blessed, and all my needs are supplied according to Your riches in glory. Let joy, peace, prosperity, and success be as abundant in my life as the stars. Your blessings, Lord, make me rich, and everything I need to fulfill my destiny will be at my disposal when I need it. In the name of Jesus, amen.

March 19

Charge the Atmosphere With Praise

Now when they began to sing and to praise, the Lord *set ambushes against the people of Ammon, Moab, and Mount Seir, who had come against Judah; and they were defeated.*
—2 Chronicles 20:22

Rather than being afraid, Jehoshaphat got God's plan and put it into action. He took God at His word that the battle was His. Then they celebrated God's salvation before they even saw it. They filled their atmosphere with praise and worship, charging the air with God's power and provision, and by the time they saw their enemies, their enemies were already defeated.

I declare that I am already victorious in You. Sin has no dominion over me. My past has no dominion over me. I am more than a conqueror through You. Nothing can separate me from Your love. If You are for me, nothing and no one can be against me. The enemy will not triumph over me. Your plans and purposes will prevail. In Jesus's name, amen.

Agree With God

Let us hold fast the confession of our hope without wavering, for He who promised is faithful.
—Hebrews 10:23

Come into agreement with what God has already said in His Word about you and your situation. You have to get God's Word on it. Then fill your atmosphere with His promises on the matter.

Father, sanctify me with Your truth; Your Word is truth. I fill my mind with Your Word. It is a lamp unto my feet and a light unto my path. Order my steps in Your Word, so I don't stumble or fall. I stand in agreement with what You have said. No weapon formed against me shall prosper. You are fighting my battles, and victory is on the way. Father, help me to walk in the truth that sets me free. In Jesus's name, amen.

March 21

Bring It Forth

By faith we understand that the worlds were framed by the word of God, so that the things which are seen were not made of things which are visible.
—Hebrews 11:3

Anything you are able to see was made from that which is not seen. This is an amazing concept, and it is what makes the biblical truths about spiritual reality so fascinating. There is nothing that currently exists that has not always been. That means whatever you are able to experience with your five senses was "brought forth" from the spiritual realm; it was made manifest by the power of God, and it's that same power that works in and through you. I say "made manifest" because that is how creation works. Knowing there is a cause for every effect, we know something "is" because it has been "brought forth." Without a thing being conceived in the mind and spoken out—without calling those things that are not as though they were—nothing that exists would exist.

Father, I align my words with Your Word and my will with Your will. I declare today that my vision is clear, my mission is unobstructed, and I make a difference in the world. I decree and declare that Your power is manifest in my life. Thank You for the marvelous things You are doing, and will continue to do, in my life. In Jesus's name, amen.

Thoughts and Words Frame Reality

For by Him all things were created that are in heaven and that are on earth, visible and invisible.... All things were created through Him and for Him. And He is before all things, and in Him all things consist.

—Colossians 1:16–17

The principle of thought and word framing reality is found from the first book of the Bible to the last. It is in the story of Creation. It is in the new heaven and the new earth that are to come. God created the tangible, temporal world by calling it forth. He gave form to what physicists have come to call "substance"—the "essential nature," as *Webster's Dictionary* says, that makes up the unseen world—by changing the composition of raw energy with the power of His decrees and declarations. God didn't bring the world into being from nothingness; rather, He brought everything into existence from matter that already existed within Himself.

Father, by Your word the worlds were framed, and by Your Word my world is framed. You made me and You know me. You know my innermost thoughts. You know the desires of my heart, and You know what I am uniquely fashioned to do, because You put those capabilities within me. I run to Your Word for guidance, and You lead and guide me into all truth. I put my trust solely in You. In Jesus's name, amen.

Tap Into Unlimited Power

In the beginning God created the heavens and the earth.
—Genesis 1:1

The Latin root of *creation* is literally "to bring forth." Through the power of His thoughts and words God "brought forth" what was in Him out into the physical world.

So rather than thinking about the process of creation as making something out of nothing, for our benefit we should think of it as tapping into an unlimited source of power in the spiritual realm to bring forth what we have imagined possible. God set the universe in motion by changing His intention, focusing His thoughts, and harnessing His words. Though it is to a lesser extent, we create our personal universe in the same way.

Father, thank You for filling me with Your Spirit and allowing me to sense Your presence today. I declare that my soul is filled with joy and peace, and my heart is filled with courage. The light of Your Word illuminates my path. I decree and declare that Your plans and purposes will prevail in my life. My best and most blessed days are yet to come. My future is not defined by my past. You have begun a new thing in me. I am being transformed by the renewing of my mind. In Jesus's name, amen.

Activate Spiritual Molecules

For whatever is born of God overcomes the world. And this is the victory that has overcome the world—our faith.
—1 John 5:4

Invisible to our naked eye are the molecules hydrogen and oxygen, yet through a chemical reaction they become a visible substance called water. The same happens with sodium and chloride coming together to form table salt. God set these invisible processes in motion at creation to respond continuously to His word to form visible substances that add to our lives. He has done the same in the spiritual realm. Every moment of every day, we are surrounded by spiritual "molecules" that are designed to respond to our thoughts and intentions—or more scripturally put, our faith—to produce miracles. Everything you need for victory already exists, but it exists in another form. Since the spirit realm is the causal realm, then your miracle is always in motion—you just need to get it to manifest on your behalf!

Thank You for having already provided everything I need for my kingdom assignment. Teach me how to access the resources You have put at my disposal. I refuse to settle for anything less than Your best. It is my pleasure to do Your will. Let Your kingdom come and Your will be done. In Jesus's name, amen.

March 25

Multiply by Blessing

He took the five loaves and the two fish, and looking up to heaven, He blessed and broke and gave the loaves to the disciples; and the disciples gave to the multitudes. So they all ate and were filled, and they took up twelve baskets full of the fragments that remained.
—Matthew 14:19–20

Jesus multiplied the bread and the fish by speaking to it and blessing it. He turned His eyes toward heaven and spoke out a blessing. The verb for *bless* here means "to invoke God's presence" as well as "to infuse His provision into a thing." Jesus invoked God's presence, and the bread and fish were "brought forth" or "made manifest"—Jesus affected the spiritual "molecules" enough to cause the bread and fish to miraculously appear—but they had been there the whole time in the spiritual realm.

Lord, give me prophetic discernment that I may call forth all the things You have set aside for me. Place upon me Samuel's anointing for sensitivity and obedience to the voice of God, and Issachar's anointing for discerning the correct times and seasons. I decree and declare that I will apprehend that for which I was apprehended of Christ. In the name of Jesus I declare that I will possess everything God desires for me in its proper time. Amen.

Don't Stop Warring in Prayer

Do not fear, Daniel, for from the first day that you set your heart to understand, and to humble yourself before your God, your words were heard; and I have come because of your words.
—Daniel 10:12

When Daniel prayed, God sent the answer immediately, but there were forces that prohibited it from being manifested right away. We read in the next verse the angel's explanation for the delay: "The prince of the kingdom of Persia withstood me twenty-one days" (v. 13). As Daniel had persisted in prayer, the angel had persisted in his warring. Even though Daniel did not see any sign of the answer manifesting, it was in motion. Eventually it did come into being because Daniel never stopped praying and decreeing. The answer broke through because Daniel stood firm in his faith and his confession. Remember, there are always forces at work prohibiting your answer from manifesting. If you don't sabotage your prayers with negative thoughts and words, then you will eventually see with your eyes the substance of what you have hoped for, just as Daniel did.

I stand in faith today, knowing that the answers I seek are on their way. I will be like the persistent widow and keep on asking, keep on knocking, and keep on seeking. I will not grow weary in prayer, for in due season I shall reap if I faint not. In the name of Jesus, amen.

Seeds Take Time

By faith, Noah built a ship in the middle of dry land. He was warned about something he couldn't see, and acted on what he was told. The result? His family was saved. His act of faith drew a sharp line between the evil of the unbelieving world and the rightness of the believing world. As a result, Noah became intimate with God.

—Hebrews 11:7, The Message

A seed buried in the ground can go weeks without an apparent change before it sprouts. The fact that we don't see the seed doesn't mean it isn't there. So many times we declare a thing and then lose patience because it doesn't manifest like popcorn in a microwave. Just because we don't see a thing come to pass in a certain period of time doesn't mean it isn't ever going to be or that it isn't God's will. Sometimes it takes time. We need to believe and speak as if it is coming today but persist in our faith even if it takes decades. We can undo what we have set in motion if we choose to speak words of discouragement instead of words filled with faith

I remind myself of Your faithfulness, and my faith grows. I will not give place to doubt. Though the promise tarry, I will wait for it. It shall come to pass in due season. In the name of Jesus, amen.

Let Your Words Incubate

Let the words of my mouth and the meditation of my heart be acceptable in Your sight, O Lord, *my strength and my Redeemer.*
—Psalm 19:14

Words don't just disappear once they are released into the atmosphere. They remain dormant there, incubating until the time for them to bear fruit is at hand. It could be they will be activated by someone else who will trigger a catalyst in the realm of the spirit in order for what you are hoping for to be made manifest. It could be there are opposing forces that require your perseverance. It could be any number of things delaying what God wants for you, but God kept it simple: regardless of the *why*, you need to keep your thoughts, your words, and your faith in line with what you are expecting, and then trust God to take care of the rest.

Lord, I fix my eyes on You. I will not be moved by my circumstances. I will not turn to the right or to the left. I will wait on You to fulfill Your promises. You are a faithful God, and You are not slow in keeping Your promises as some understand slowness. Because I keep my mind stayed on You, I remain in perfect peace. In Jesus's name, amen.

Be Bold in Faith

Caleb interrupted, called for silence before Moses and said, "Let's go up and take the land—now. We can do it."
—Numbers 13:30, The Message

It was fear alone that caused the Israelites to miss out on the promise of God. Instead of inheriting property, they were forced to wander homeless until the next generation rose up bold enough to take possession and move in. Among those allowed to become property owners were Joshua and Caleb, the only two of the former generation given the right to hold title and deed in the land of promise. When the Israelites cried out in fear before Moses, it was Caleb who spoke up, saying, "Let's go at once to take the land. We can certainly conquer it!" God honored Caleb's faith.

I know that with You all things are possible. Through You I can take the "land" and conquer new territories. I will not be afraid of the giants. You are greater than any obstacle I face. Through You I am supernaturally fashioned for victory. I arise boldly and declare victory over every enemy that would seek to thwart the plans and purposes of God. Your kingdom is my priority; I delight in doing Your will. In the name of Jesus, amen.

Attract the Attention of Angels

Do you think that I cannot appeal to my Father, and he will at once send me more than twelve legions of angels?
—Matthew 26:53, esv

Fallen angels cause deviations to what God originally purposed. They operate much like the heavenly angels assigned to bring about the manifestation to your prayers, only in the exact opposite way. When they fell from heaven, their mission became perverted—so instead of bringing answers, they prohibit answers from manifesting. Your faith attracts the attention of heaven's angels to work on your behalf, while your fear draws the demons of hell to work against you. Your words become the magnet that draws either heaven or hell into your situation. But always remember: no force is more powerful than the spoken Word of God.

Lord, You give Your angels charge over me to keep me in all my ways. Satan comes only to steal, kill, and destroy, but You have come that I may have life and that more abundantly. I will not play into the enemy's hands by giving place to fear and anxiety. I will proclaim Your Word, because Your angels respond to Your Word. According to Psalm 34:7, let Your angels encamp round about me now and, Lord, deliver me in Jesus's name. Amen.

Tune In to God's Frequency

Then [Jacob] dreamed, and behold, a ladder was set up on the earth, and its top reached to heaven; and there the angels of God were ascending and descending on it. And behold, the Lord stood above it and said: "I am the Lord God of Abraham your father and the God of Isaac; the land on which you lie I will give to you and your descendants.... Then Jacob awoke from his sleep and said, "Surely the Lord is in this place, and I did not know it."

—Genesis 28:12–16

God gave Jacob a vision where he saw a ladder going up to heaven—the top of the ladder touched heaven and the bottom touched the earth. There were angels ascending and descending—much like radio waves moving along an antenna. This is exactly how divine inspiration works. Here God was speaking to Jacob's mind and enabling him to pick up a spiritual frequency. When he got tuned in to this frequency, he saw how the invisible realm was manifesting itself in the visible realm. So too can you.

Father, sharpen my spiritual discernment so I will know Your voice. Grant me the ability to hear clearly as You give me insight into Your plans. Cause my spiritual eyes to function with 20/20 vision for the correct understanding of the times and seasons. In Jesus's name, amen.

April

April 1

See What Already Exists

The secret things belong to the Lord our God, but those things which are revealed belong to us and our children forever, that we may do all the words of this law.
—Deuteronomy 29:29

God gave Moses a vision of something that already existed in heaven—the actual spiritual tabernacle. He opened the eyes of Moses, and Moses was able to see it and replicate it here on the earth. Secret things belong to God, but those things that are revealed belong to man. It is a point of revelation—a point of inspiration—where God wants to speak to us all. He knows the end from the beginning, and He knows everything in between—and those are the things that He wants to reveal to you.

Thank You, Lord, for revelation knowledge. Place upon me Paul's anointing for cutting-edge apostolic revelation and Elijah's anointing for prophetic accuracy and insights. Anoint me to discern the correct times and seasons, and give me divine strategy for each new season. Open my spiritual eyes so that the spirit dimension is more real to me than the natural. Teach me Your ways so that I walk in Your wisdom and supernatural discernment. In Jesus's name, amen.

Do Your Part to Bring It Forth

Eye has not seen, nor ear heard, nor have entered into the heart of man the things which God has prepared for those who love Him.
—1 Corinthians 2:9

In Job 38 God is asking Job a series of questions. At one point God asks, "Where were you…when the morning stars sang together?" (vv. 4, 7). Later He inquires, "Have you commanded the morning since your days began?" (v. 12). In a sense God is asking Job, "Have you thought about speaking into your morning and bringing order into your day?" If these things are prepared but we have not received them, it could mean we have not done our part in bringing them forth.

Father, I arise today in Your strength, ready to be a blessing to my friends, family, community, and nation. I know that I am not here by accident. You had a plan for me before I was even born, a plan that I will fulfill. I commit to being diligent so I will receive the full reward You have prepared for me. Lord, bless the works of my hands. Let my name be associated with good things. Shield me from persecution and false accusations; guard me against greed, discouragement, and sabotage. I welcome opportunities to grow and mature. Let my actions be in sync with Your will. In Jesus's name, amen.

April 3

Move Out in Obedience

By faith, Abraham, at the time of testing, offered Isaac back to God. Acting in faith, he was as ready to return the promised son, his only son, as he had been to receive him—and this after he had already been told, "Your descendants shall come from Isaac."

—Hebrews 11:17–18, The Message

God said He wanted Abraham to sacrifice his most precious treasure—his son Isaac. As they moved toward the place of sacrifice, as Abraham lifted his hand to carry out God's instructions, there appeared a ram caught in the thicket. God provided the alternative, but not until Abraham moved out in obedience. The provision would not have appeared had Abraham not taken the first step. Many times God is expecting the corresponding action from us in order to bring these things to pass. What are you doing to prepare for the thing you have been declaring and believing for? How do your actions correspond to your belief that a certain event will come to pass as a result of the integrity of God's Word?

To the faithful You show Yourself faithful, so I will be faithful to You and Your Word. I will obey Your instructions. You have shown Yourself faithful time and again. So I will trust You, even when I don't understand what You're doing. I will follow You without complaint. In Jesus's name, amen.

Don't Underestimate Your Strength

You are a chosen generation, a royal priest-hood, a holy nation, His own special people.
—1 Peter 2:9

A king does not ask for anything—a king declares his decrees because he has that authority, and those in his world rush to see that they are accomplished. Don't ever think that you are a weak, defeated victim. You are a royal priesthood adorned with a kingly anointing. Never underestimate the strength that resides in you through Christ. You command a power to change the course of your destiny that the great heroes of the Old Testament could only dream of.

Father, I am part of a chosen generation, a royal priesthood, a holy nation. I am not rendered powerless. I establish a breakthrough atmosphere in the name of Jesus. Father, heal the land of civil unrest, human trafficking, pandemic disease, homelessness, and every ungodly work. Turn the economic tides in our favor and bring increase. Bring into office leaders who are free of corruption. Remove those who are driven by selfish ambition and greed. Replace them with servant leaders. Father, in You we have hope. In Jesus's name, amen.

April 5

Activate Your Blessing

You will make your prayer to Him, He will hear you, and you will pay your vows. You will also declare a thing, and it will be established for you; so light will shine on your ways.
—Job 22:27–28

Just as God declares a thing, He expects you, as king and priest, to do the same. Another way to say it is that His blessings are voice activated. To "make your prayer" means "to construct." You are going to construct your prayers. You are going to decree what God has put on your heart to desire.

You desire good things for me, and I align my speech with the good plans You have for my life. I decree and declare that my day will fully cooperate with Your will. I have fresh excitement to serve You in holiness and righteousness, and my name is associated with integrity and wisdom. I walk in divine health, and I eat the good of the land. No weapon formed against me shall prosper. Let every evil spirit seeking to frustrate my day and my assignment be thwarted. In the name of Jesus, amen.

April 6

Head True North

Guard your heart above all else, for it determines the course of your life.
—Proverbs 4:23, NLT

The patriarchs of Israel attempted to change the trajectory of their lives or their nation. Jacob wrestled. Lot inquired. Moses intervened. David repented. Solomon asked. Daniel fasted. They strove and pled and fought for the right to influence their destiny—a destiny you have been given the privilege to shape simply by giving the word. Make sure that as you take command, you are heading true north by diligently guarding your heart and staying on heaven's course.

Teach me to hide Your Word in my heart so I will not sin against You. I know I will keep my way pure by living according to Your Word. Let me not stray from Your commands. Cause Your Word to change the way I think, the way I speak, and the way I live. I commit to seek You with all my heart. In the name of Jesus, amen.

April 7

Where Are You Moving Today?

If you keep yourself pure, you will be a special utensil for honorable use. Your life will be clean, and you will be ready for the Master to use you for every good work.
—2 Timothy 2:21, NLT

Our future comes one day at a time—it is God's present to you. Every moment of every day, with every thought you think and word you speak, you are making a decision to move toward greatness or obscurity. If you are to make the most of every opportunity you are given, you must learn to harness and then maximize the potential of your thoughts and words. If you are to become the champion God has created you to be, you must create a royal priestly mind-set by practicing noble thought habits and disciplining your tongue to speak success-filled words.

I decree and declare that I am purposely built and uniquely designed for success. I am free in Christ, and by His stripes I am healed physically, emotionally, and every other way a person can be healed. I am Christ's workmanship, created in Him for good works. Father, according to Hebrews 10:22, I decree and declare that I am drawing near to You with a true heart in full assurance of faith, having my heart sprinkled from an evil conscience and my body washed with pure water. Let Your Word renew my mind so I can become more like You. In Jesus's name, amen.

April 8

Prayers Can Multiply

Five of you shall chase a hundred, and a hundred of you shall put ten thousand to flight; your enemies shall fall by the sword before you.
—Leviticus 26:8

When hearts gather together and unite, the force of the prayer is multiplied exponentially in the Spirit. No matter how many are assembled, these prayers ascend as multiples of hundreds and thousands for each person present. When we gather together to pray, there is a corporate anointing that harnesses the prayer of agreement to bind, loose, tear down, pluck up, and sound the trumpet for spiritual advancement. The foundations of the earth are shaken by corporate prayer, shaking whatever can be shaken, so only that which cannot be shaken will remain. All flesh and diabolical schemes are overridden. The threats and whispers of the adversary are silenced and annihilated as we pray.

I stand in agreement with believers around the world who want to see Your kingdom come and Your will done on the earth. Let us fulfill our spiritual and social contracts with the world and empower us to live true to our core values and Christ's principles in the earth, especially in the marketplace. In Jesus's name, amen.

April 9

Align Yourself With God's Word

Look carefully then how you walk! Live purposefully and worthily and accurately, not as the unwise and witless, but as wise (sensible, intelligent people), making the very most of the time [buying up each opportunity], because the days are evil. Therefore do not be vague and thoughtless and foolish, but understanding and firmly grasping what the will of the Lord is.

—Ephesians 5:15–17, amp

We must be intentional and purposeful with how we use all of the resources at our disposal. The key to making the most of every opportunity is to grasp firmly the will of the Lord. This is why it is vitally important to renew your mind continually with the Word of God. You must daily align your thoughts and words with God's.

I decree and declare that my destiny is aligned with Your perfect will. My actions are synchronized with the rhythms of heaven. I fill my mind with Your Word so that it may illuminate my path. Thank You for the assurance that You are in control and that I am loved, blessed, and highly favored. I put my earnest expectation and my hope in You. Thank You for transforming me by the power of Your Word. In Jesus's name, amen.

What Do You Trust?

And all the children of Israel complained against Moses and Aaron, and the whole congregation said to them, "If only we had died in the land of Egypt! Or if only we had died in this wilderness! Why has the Lord brought us to this land to fall by the sword, that our wives and children should become victims? Would it not be better for us to return to Egypt?"

—Numbers 14:2–3

God had spoken good things over the people of Israel and promised to give them the land of Canaan for their inheritance. However, they trusted more in their own fears than in God. They trusted more in the comfort of slavery than in the hope of living as kings and priests. Though God had promised them their own land, they undid His promises not only with their lack of faith but also with the words they spoke. Let this not be true of you.

Father, let the words of my mouth and the meditations of my heart be acceptable in Your sight. I will not fear new territory because I am called to influence others. I commit to bear Your light as a change agent in the world. I decree and declare that I trust You and do not doubt. I will not second-guess what You have said, for Your Word is truth. In Jesus's name, amen.

April 11

Order Your Day

Teach us to number our days, that we may gain a heart of wisdom.
—Psalm 90:12

We must all learn the art of ordering our day. We are to take into account each day and not squander the time that we have. Wisdom redeems the time and makes the most of every opportunity. It seems simple, but seemingly innocuous time wasters are one of the enemy's most effective tools in keeping the body of Christ "off task."

I decree and declare that I make the most of my time. I do not procrastinate. I act now, without hesitation, anxiety, or fear. I walk in Your timing. Father, cause me to know my end and what is the measure of my days; let me realize how fleeting my time on earth is! My days are but a few handbreadths. Let my heart keep Your command, for they will add length of days, long life, and peace to me. In Jesus's name, amen.

April 12

What's Most Important?

See then that you walk circumspectly, not as fools but as wise, redeeming the time, because the days are evil.
—Ephesians 5:15–16

Ordering your day requires the ability to prioritize. It requires the ability to discern what is distracting busywork and what is kingdom business. Effective time management requires getting God's heart on what is worth investing time in versus what we should not be spending or even wasting time on. As with any financial investment, you must ask what kind of return your time investments are yielding. Time "spent" is a cost—and you must be mindful of the benefit you are exchanging for the cost you are incurring.

Unless You build the house, I labor in vain. Give me wisdom to order this day according to Your perfect plan. I will not follow my own agenda. Let Your Spirit be with me—before me, behind me, when I speak, when I rise, and in all my dealings today. Teach me how to improve my productivity—to work smarter and more efficiently. I work as unto You. Let mutually beneficial relationships, favor, affluence, influence, happiness, support, beauty, purpose, direction, and abundant living be my constant companions today. In Jesus's name, amen.

April 13

Tune In to God's Rhythm

The heavens declare the glory of God; and the firmament shows His handiwork. Day unto day utters speech, and night unto night reveals knowledge.
—Psalm 19:1–2

We experience that God is a God of order by the consistency of seasons, tides, and solar orbits. We can order our lives because we know with what accuracy the sun will set and rise again, how the seasons will change, the tides will turn, and the planets will rotate on their axes. There is a cadence and rhythm to our lives because of the order God has put into place through the universe in which we are suspended and the nature within which we dwell. From ecosystems to solar systems, God has set into motion patterns that we can study and document through what we call science.

Thank You for bringing order into my life. Where there had been chaos and pain, You have brought discipline and healing. Where there had been defeat, You have brought victory. Where there had been lack, You have brought abundance. You have provided all I need for life and godliness, and You will not stop now. Release angelic escorts to safely lead me where You would have me go. Cause my will to work in perfect harmony with Yours. In Jesus's name, amen.

How Is God's Order Your Own?

Starting from scratch, [God] made the entire human race and made the earth hospitable, with plenty of time and space for living so we could seek after God, and not just grope around in the dark but actually find him.

—Acts 17:26, The Message

God provided the ultimate example of effective time management and order in the Book of Genesis. In six days He created the earth and everything in it, and on the seventh day He rested. It all went according to plan. There was an order to when and how He created what and when—a succession and progression to how He developed each organism and species. God did not waste His resources, and He especially did not waste His time. He was purposeful and concise as He unfolded life on our planet.

Surely, God, You bring about Your purposes for me. Before I was even born, You knew me. You knew the number of my days and all that I was created to do. You have called me for a righteous purpose, and You take me by the hand and lead me into my destiny. I decree and declare this year is pregnant with purpose. It is filled with promise, and I am fully equipped to accomplish all that You have for me to do. In Jesus's name, amen.

April 15

Are You Disciplined?

Be sure that everything is done properly and in order.
—1 Corinthians 14:40, NLT

Look at Noah, Joseph, Moses, and David. All were men of honor and order. They were disciplined and dedicated, and they submitted themselves to God's commands. They were bold and courageous because they understood the power of a divine hierarchy and authority. They followed orders, knowing the power available in submitting to God. Even Solomon understood the importance of order when he meticulously followed God's instructions and chain of command in building the temple. We read in 2 Chronicles 8:16, "Now all the work of Solomon was well-ordered from the day of the foundation of the house of the Lord until it was finished."

Father, You have given me great authority, but I submit myself totally to You. Like the centurion in Matthew 8, I am a person of authority under authority, and I know that when You speak the word, change happens. I put my trust completely in You, because You are more than able to accomplish all that concerns me today. Even if I try to make plans, You have the final word and determine my steps. Lead me in the way I should go. I will not take one step without You. In Jesus's name, amen.

April 16

Bring Order to Your World

A land as dark as darkness itself, as the shadow of death, without any order, where even the light is like darkness.
—Job 10:22

Order is a condition in which freedom from disorder or disruption is maintained through structures, systems, and protocol. Whenever there is a lack of order, rank, or command chain; whenever protocol is not present; or whenever a code of conduct is not perceived or understood, it brings about emptiness, and lack of purpose and meaning. If your life is characterized by confusion, conflict, frustration, or lack of direction, meaning, or insight, it is an indication that you are deficient in the area of order. Where there is no order, there is no light.

With Your word You brought order out of chaos. You said, "Let there be light," and there was light. Let there be light and order in my life and in my day. A person without discipline is like a city left without walls. I will not leave my defenses down. I close every entryway the enemy might use to frustrate my day and my future. I decree and declare that my life is not characterized by confusion, frustration, or lack of direction. It is marked by vision, power, love, productivity, and purposefulness. In Jesus's name, amen.

April 17

Make Things Happen

Teach us to number our days, that we may gain a heart of wisdom.
—Psalm 90:12

Until you decide to reverse the perpetual cycle of disorder, you will continue to experience cycles of defeat and failure. This principle is illustrated by the law of entropy—the tendency of energy to dissipate and go from a state of order to one of disorder. Entropy can be defined as a dispersal of energy. Unless you intentionally harness time and energy, unless you command it with the authority you have been given, your life will dissolve into a state of chaos, and you will never experience the life of significance and fruitfulness God has purposed for you. Don't just let things happen; make things happen.

I take authority over my life and my day. I will no longer experience cycles of defeat. I will not wander aimlessly through life. I align my words and my will with Your Word. I meditate on Your Word and allow it to renew my mind; therefore, I take sure steps on a solid foundation of truth. I walk in success and prosperity. I have a fresh anointing. No more frustration. No more defeat. No more hopelessness and despair. Thank You, Father, for doing a new thing in me. In Jesus's name, amen.

April 18

Order Creates Peace and Freedom

For everything there is a season, a time for every activity under heaven.
—Ecclesiastes 3:1, NLT

Do not miss out on the rewards of well-managed time. Order is what gives you the freedom to be creative. Order gives you the peace of mind you need to tune in to God's supernatural frequencies and tap into divine inspiration. Without order you will be distracted with the cares and concerns of this life so that you cannot still your mind to hear God's voice. It is impossible to imagine and envision when you are overextended and stressed. You need to schedule time to purposefully paint the canvas of your life by investing in creative dreaming. Stop to think. Order your day so that you have the time and peace you need to create the masterpiece God has preordained for you.

Father, place upon me Deborah's anointing for balance. Show me what activities can be removed from my schedule or delegated to someone else. I never want to be too busy to sit at Your feet and learn from You. Holy Spirit, as I spend time with You, download creative ideas. Empower me to excel in my profession. Show me the cause I was created to champion. I seek You first, because then all these things will be added to me. In Jesus's name, amen.

April 19

Give Yourself Time

Put God in charge of your work, then what you've planned will take place.
—Proverbs 16:3, The Message

Like any professional composer, artist, architect, writer, or programmer, you must schedule time to think things through. Form follows thought, and the shape of your life is a product of that thought. Structure your time so you can structure your thoughts, for they provide the structure for your life. Know when to take hold of an idea and run with it and when to wait and let it mature until it has ripened. Get God's timing. Discern God's order.

For everything there is a season and a time for every purpose under heaven. Download success, prosperity, health, vision, direction, ingenuity, righteousness, peace, and resourcefulness from Your Spirit into my day. Open windows of divine inspiration, and give me eyes to see cutting-edge technologies, tactics, and strategies that can multiply my productivity and fruitfulness. Grant me the ability to hear You clearly as You give me witty inventions and creative ideas. I commit my ways to You. I will not despise what seems like a delay. I know that You have begun a good work in me, and You will complete it. In Jesus's name, amen.

April 20

God's Kind of Resurrection

If you don't know what you're doing, pray to the Father. He loves to help. You'll get his help, and won't be condescended to when you ask for it. Ask boldly, believingly, without a second thought.
—James 1:5–6, The Message

When you pray, don't let yourself waver in your faith. Hold fast to what you have learned and the confidence you have received in your relationship with Christ, even in things thought to be dead and buried, irreversible or impossible. God can resurrect a life thought to be over. He can heal the terminally ill, save the worst of sinners, and topple tyrannical governments. You acknowledge His ability to cause dead things to live when you are faithful in prayer. When you hold your place in faith, continuing to believe God, God is pleased, breakthroughs are secured, divine interventions are guaranteed, and eternal life is apprehended for you and those you pray for.

Father, nothing is too hard for You. Just as Ezekiel spoke to the valley of dry bones, I speak to dead hopes, dead dreams, and impossible situations and command them to live in the name of Jesus. The situation is not over until You say it's over, so I refuse to lose heart. I declare that my faith will not fail. I will ask You boldly, believing, without a second thought, and expect You to move on my behalf. In Jesus's name, amen.

April 21

Ease Your Load

The steps of a good man are ordered by the Lord, and He delights in his way.
—Psalm 37:23

It may seem like a daunting—if not exhausting—task to establish a greater degree of order in your life. That may feel impossible if you feel you are already overstretched. But taking time to order your day should not be an additional burden or one more "to do" on your list of duties and responsibilities. Order will ease your load and free your mind for greater peace, joy, and creativity. By more effectively ordering your day, you will gain a sense of control, a sense of purpose, increased productivity, an environment of creativity, and a greater focus and flow of accomplishments.

Father, I anticipate the good things You have prepared for me today. Bring complete order to my day as I seek You first and make Your will my priority. I rejoice in the new day You have given me. I praise You for making it fruitful and productive. Thank You for teaching me ways to increase my effectiveness—to work smarter. I work according to Your agenda and perform for an audience of one—the Lord Jesus Christ. In Jesus's name, amen.

April 22

Move Toward Stillness

Now may the Lord of peace himself give you peace at all times in every way.
—2 Thessalonians 3:16, esv

You may be looking at your life and wondering if it is possible to remove the cloud of chaos that seems to hold dominion over you. There are two simple things you can do in order to move toward clearer skies. First, unclutter your environment. Whether at home or at the office, tidy up your immediate surroundings. When you have cleared off your desk or straightened your bedroom, wherever you find yourself, stop for a moment and unclutter your mind. Pause and still your thoughts so you can gain clarity on what is the most important thing for you to focus upon in your present moment.

Father, I decree and declare that I will be anxious for nothing. But in everything by prayer and supplication with thanksgiving, I will make my requests known to You. I arise in faith today knowing that You hear and answer prayer. Because I bring my needs to You, I will walk in the peace of God that surpasses understanding, and it will guard my heart and mind. In stillness and quietness I will wait for You, and You will lead me in the way I should go. I seal these declarations in the name of Jesus, amen.

April 23

Create Pockets of Peace

For God is not a God of confusion but of peace.
—1 Corinthians 14:33, ESV

Don't wait until every area of your external environment is completely organized, but create pockets of order where you can clear your mind and order your thoughts. Your immediate environment and the atmosphere you create will go far to enhance the order you are able to establish in your sphere of influence. Practice clearing your head by journaling or meditating on Scripture. Find a space where you can usher in the peace of God by quieting your mind through worship. Dump the distractions that try and push their way into your inner sanctuary by making lists and putting plans on paper to do later. Corral all those rogue thoughts onto a piece of paper where they can remain until you are ready to address them.

In stillness and quietness I find strength, so I wait on You, Lord. I meditate on Your goodness and love. Insignificant things will not distract me; I will spend time with You. Let the zeal of the Lord fill my spirit. Let my mouth be filled with Your praise and my soul with Your joy and peace. I will not be anxious because I know You are with me. In Jesus's name, amen.

April 24

Take Dominion Over Your Day

The Lord our God broke out against us, because we did not consult Him about the proper order.
—1 Chronicles 15:13

Getting God's order for every area of our lives is serious business. We serve a God of order. The enemy uses disorder and confusion to wreak destruction. God calls you to follow after peace and righteousness to establish order and freedom. Take dominion over your day, your environment, and your destiny by setting things in their proper order. Seek the Lord early and consult Him about ordering your day aright!

Father, reveal to me Your proper order for this day that I may walk in Your blessing and favor. You delight in every detail of my life, and You establish my steps. I fear You, Lord, and I know You will instruct me in the way I should choose. Father, align every facet of this day with Your original plan and purpose for me. In the name of Jesus, amen.

April 25

Will You Wake Early?

O God, You are my God; early will I seek You; my soul thirsts for You; my flesh longs for You in a dry and thirsty land where there is no water.
—Psalm 63:1

The Bible is full of references to God's prophets and saints rising early to pray or hear God's voice. God is notorious for waking His followers early in the morning to give them instructions, insights, or warnings. Those who seek to be used of God must be willing to rise up early. Soldiers are ever alert and ready to respond to orders. The bugle blows early because battles are won through the preparations done in the early hours of the day—especially spiritual battles. Learn to love the dawn, for there is power in the rising of the Son!

"Let the morning bring me word of your unfailing love, for I have put my trust in you. Show me the way I should go, for to you I lift up my soul" (Ps. 143:8, NIV*). Your thoughts about me are so precious, Father. I look forward to spending time with You at the start of each day, worshipping You and meditating on Your Word. My soul thirsts for You, Lord. Empower me to serve You in holiness and righteousness. In Jesus's name, amen.*

April 26

Praise Your Way to Victory

So they rose early in the morning and went out into the Wilderness of Tekoa; and as they went out, Jehoshaphat stood and said, "Hear me, O Judah and you inhabitants of Jerusalem: Believe in the Lord your God, and you shall be established; believe His prophets, and you shall prosper."

—2 Chronicles 20:20

In 2 Chronicles God promises the Israelites victory against their enemies. He tells them not to be afraid of the multitudes, for He will fight the battle for them. He instructs the Israelites to position themselves and to stand firm. The Lord says to them, "Do not fear or be dismayed; tomorrow go out against them, for the Lord is with you" (2 Chron. 20:17). They rose early and began to sing and praise the Lord. As they sang praises to God, the Lord caused confusion among the enemy camp, and their foes turned on each other until all of them were utterly destroyed. The Israelites spent the next three days carrying away the spoil that was left behind. Good things come to those who rise early and praise God.

I lift my voice to praise You today. I will not be silent because I can't help but remember Your goodness. Let Your praise continually be in my mouth. I know that my praise silences the accuser. I stand firm in faith, trusting You until the battle is won. In Jesus's name, amen.

April 27

Rise Early to Seek the Lord

Awake, my glory! Awake, lute and harp! I will awaken the dawn.
—Psalm 57:8

The Bible records that David was Israel's greatest warrior, king, poet, and prophet. He was one of Scripture's most passionate and purposeful characters, and he left an enduring legacy of victory, wisdom, and significance. What set David apart? What caused David to become an enduring hero of the faith? He rose early to seek the Lord.

As David did, I will seek You with my whole heart. "In the morning, O Lord, you hear my voice; in the morning I lay my requests before you and wait in expectation" (Ps. 5:3, NIV). I decree and declare that I have a well-instructed tongue to know the word that sustains me because You awaken me morning by morning to hear Your instructions. Father, show me Your power today. Let Your favor be upon me and establish the work of my hands. Make my feet like hinds' feet over all my troubles. Lead me along paths of righteousness. In the name of Jesus, amen.

April 28

Follow the Example of Jesus

At daybreak Jesus went out to a solitary place.
—Luke 4:42, NIV

Jesus, in whom God said He was well pleased, habitually rose early to pray: "Now in the morning, having risen a long while before daylight, He went out and departed to a solitary place; and there He prayed" (Mark 1:35). If the Lord Jesus Christ had to rise early to pray, how much more should we begin our day in prayer?

Father, I long to become more like Jesus. I want to reflect His character and walk in the strength of His power. It is Your will for me to be conformed to the image of Your Son. You are the potter; I am the clay. Mold me. Shape my will so that it aligns with Yours. Teach me to love others as You have loved us. In Jesus's name, amen.

April 29

Change the State of the World

I, even I, am He who blots out your transgressions for My own sake; and I will not remember your sins. Put Me in remembrance; let us contend together; state your case, that you may be acquitted.
—Isaiah 43:25–26

God has given a mandate that we are to invoke His name to cause needed changes in lives and communities. This mandate gives us the confidence by which we can pray with authority—in effect arguing court cases before the judgment seat of heaven. As members of planet Earth's true parliament, we are representatives before the Great Judge, advocates lobbying heaven for change on the earth. We have the legitimate authority to speak to God on behalf of the earth and for the sake of humankind.

I decree and declare that the plans and purpose of God will prevail in my life, my community, and my nation. Your kingdom shall come and Your will shall be done on earth as it is in heaven. The anointing of God breaks every yoke. Place Your anointing on me, and let there be a breakthrough in the heavens. Father, assign angels to reinforce me as I advance into new levels, dimensions, realms, and territories. I am Your ambassador in the earth. I commit to bear Your light as an agent of change in a world of darkness. In Jesus's name, amen.

You Must Believe What You Pray

Whoever catches a glimpse of the revealed counsel of God—the free life!—even out of the corner of his eye, and sticks with it, is no distracted scatterbrain but a man or woman of action. That person will find delight and affirmation in the action.
—James 1:25, The Message

Let there be no misunderstanding. You can speak words in prayer that you do not believe, and they will not produce the results you are looking for. Parroting without conviction or faith does not produce divine alignment. You must be decisive. Make a deliberate and conscious decision to agree with the Word of God, and then set your heart to be convinced of the truth of what you have read or heard. Only when you are able to do that shall you attain to the higher heights and deeper depths. Once you have decided to throw your full conviction into your words, heaven and earth will align to answer your prayers.

Without faith it is impossible to please God, so I choose to walk by faith. Faith cometh by hearing and hearing the Word of God, so I will meditate on Your Word. It will not return void but will accomplish that for which it has been sent. I know that if I can believe, all things are possible. You are able to do exceeding abundantly above all that I could ask or think according to the power at work in me. So I commit to trust You and Your Word. I will not doubt. In Jesus's name, amen.

May

May 1

Get God's Special Word for You

Yes, by my spirit within me I will seek You early; for when Your judgments are in the earth, the inhabitants of the world will learn righteousness.
—Isaiah 26:9

God wants to speak into your life so that He can help you order your day with greater authority and success. Tap into God's best for you by rising early to spend time in His presence. Let the Lord fill your heart with His peace and joy, stand firm on His promises, and get His special word for you so that you can stand and declare it throughout the day. Seek wisdom; seek understanding; study to show yourself approved. Rise early, as did the prophet Isaiah, so that you will have the tongue of the wise, ready to give an answer for the hope that is in you.

I will follow hard after You. I reverently fear You and keep Your commandments. I will rise early to seek You, and I will obey Your voice. I cling to You. When I pursue You, I will be found by You. I love Your words. I can do nothing by myself. I will do only as I am taught of You. I am led by Your Spirit for I am a child of God. Thank You, Father, for guiding me into all truth. In the name of Jesus, amen.

God's Yes and Amen

For the Son of God, Jesus Christ, who was preached among you by us—by me, Silvanus, and Timothy—was not Yes and No, but in Him was Yes. For all the promises of God in Him are Yes, and in Him Amen, to the glory of God through us.
—2 Corinthians 1:19–20

People often think that when they have prayed for something once and not received it, perhaps it is because God's answer to the question was, "No, you can't have that." Paul tells us that God is a "yes" and "amen" God! Many times prayers do or don't get answered because we are simply not practiced enough in the way of prayer, or we have not given God anything to say yes or amen to. As long as you are praying His Word according to His will, God's answers to your prayer will always be yes and amen, but that is often followed with an enabling—an instruction or a word of wisdom—that is necessary to then walk the answer out.

If I ask anything according to Your will, You hear me, and I can have what I asked. Empower me to extract wisdom from Your Word; let it shape my thoughts and actions so that I walk in step with You. In the name of Jesus, amen.

May 3

Will You Be Bold?

Proclaiming the kingdom of God and teaching about the Lord Jesus Christ with all boldness and without hindrance.
—Acts 28:31, ESV

Success requires courage and boldness. It requires that you walk in genuine spiritual authority in order to take dominion over your inner and outer world. God has empowered you, through Christ, to speak light into every situation. He has given you the tools and ability to dispel the dark and create beauty and order wherever you are. Whatever lies before you can be the substance from which you call forth your own masterpiece.

I will take possession of all You have assigned to me. Father, place the anointing of a warrior upon me. I decree and declare that there will be no hindrance in my family, relationships, finances, health, or mind. I am taking new territory. My mind is filled with divinely inspired ideas. My hands are productive, and I am a history-maker for Christ. I will become all that I was born to be, in Jesus's name, amen.

May 4

You're Meant to Be an Active Participant

God said to them, "Be fruitful and multiply; fill the earth and subdue it; have dominion over the fish of the sea, over the birds of the air, and over every living thing that moves over the earth."
—Genesis 1:28

God created paradise and then gave His ultimate creation, man, the authority to rule over it. He told Adam to name every creature, calling each one out before him one at a time—thus Adam proclaimed the name of and ordered every species. Man was given dominion over all creation and the power to silence all of his enemies (Ps. 8). God didn't create mankind to be idle but rather to be an active participant in making the earth over into the form God intended. God locked up all the mysteries of what humanity would ever need in what He created, so that we could co-labor with Him to unravel those mysteries and continue moving creation toward its expected end.

Father, creation groans for the revealing of the sons of God. It is within our power to declare Your order in the earth today. Fill the atmosphere with Your glory. Heal the land and bring revival. Let Your purposes prevail in the earth. In Jesus's name, amen.

May 5

From One Glory to the Next

Observe and obey all these words which I command you, that it may go well with you and your children after you forever, when you do what is good and right in the sight of the Lord your God.
—Deuteronomy 12:28

Success is the fulfillment of divine purpose, while prosperity is having enough divine provision to overcome obstacles. Once you press out of one situation, realm, or domain, you will rise to a new level of strength with a greater capacity to influence your new situation or domain. In other words, you will go from one glory to another and from one level of strength to a greater one. When you learn to build on your experiences, adding to your faith, you will live a successful kingdom life as ambassadors of God's glorious kingdom. You will progress from one level of success and provision to another as you develop godly ability and character.

I will not give up during times of testing. I will press toward the mark, knowing that those who remain steadfast under a trial will receive the crown of life You promised to those who love You. The trying of my faith builds spiritual muscles that give me strength to get through the next trial. I decree and declare that I only progress; I do not regress. I move forward into my destiny no matter what obstacles come my way. In the name of Jesus, amen.

May 6

Partake of God's Divine Nature

But also for this very reason, giving all diligence, add to your faith virtue, to virtue knowledge, to knowledge self-control, to self-control perseverance, to perseverance godliness, to godliness brotherly kindness, and to brotherly kindness love. For if these things are yours and abound, you will be neither barren nor unfruitful in the knowledge of our Lord Jesus Christ.
—2 Peter 1:5–8

When Peter says "for this very reason," he is referring to having been called to partake of God's divine nature. As an ambassador, you are called to represent your heavenly Father in the earthly realm. You are to "re-present" Him, or "present Him again," in every avenue of secular interaction. The world has formulated an erroneous and limited concept of God, and you are called to demonstrate His greatness through your lifestyle. God has called you to be His showcase on the earth. Everything about you should reflect the glories of the kingdom, from the clothes you wear to the way you talk—everything that speaks to your station and quality of life. All should demonstrate the limitless glories of the kingdom of God!

I arise today in Your strength and declare that I am called to be a world-class leader within my sphere of influence. I bear Your light in a world of darkness. I will not let circumstances distract me from fulfilling my purpose. In Jesus's name, amen.

May 7

The Keys to the Kingdom

And I will give you the keys of the kingdom of heaven, and whatever you bind on earth will be bound in heaven, and whatever you loose on earth will be loosed in heaven.
—Matthew 16:19

You have become privy to the mystery of these kingdom principles or keys so that in this life you can walk in divine dominion. In other words, whatever you allow in the earthly realm, heaven allows, and whatever you say no to in Jesus's name, heaven will back you up by binding it. Remember, nothing leaves heaven until the request for it leaves earth. This is how powerful the spoken word is. It has the ability to open or close spiritual and heavenly doors.

I declare that this is a new day. I am breaking out of limitations in my mind, soul, and spirit. I decree and declare that every Jericho wall will come down, and I will possess all that You have for me. I command every situation and circumstance to come into divine alignment. The power and purpose of God will prevail in my life, in the name of Jesus. Amen.

Your Supernatural Authority

So shall My word be that goes forth from My mouth; it shall not return to Me void, but it shall accomplish what I please, and it shall prosper in the thing for which I sent it.
—Isaiah 55:11

As a living epistle, a carrier of the Spirit of Christ, the Word has been made flesh in you, and the God-breathed words that you speak carry a supernatural authority and creative power. Words are powerful. Words affect your destiny. One day of murmuring and complaining has the power to set you back for a year. That's a 1-to-365-day ratio. Therefore, you can't afford to release capricious words out of your mouth because the spirit realm takes every word uttered from man as a command and mandate. It does not discriminate between a jest, a joke, a desire, an order, or a decree. This is how powerful the spoken word is. Be careful not to become ensnared by your own words.

Father, I do not take lightly the power of my words. I speak light and life into my day. Illuminate the path You would have me to walk. Guide me into all truth. Bring insight and understanding that will cause me to be more productive. I declare that I will maximize my potential today as I move boldly toward my destiny, in Jesus's name. Amen.

May 9

Get Prayed Up

As often as possible Jesus withdrew to out-of-the-way places for prayer.
—Luke 5:16, The Message

There is no question that Jesus was always *prayed up*. He was connected with the Father and valued His prayer time so much that He would sneak away from the disciples without telling them so He could pray undisturbed for as long as He needed to pray. Then when He faced a situation—a blind person coming to Him for healing, for example—He knew just what to do.

Father, I want to walk in sync with You. Download Your divine instruction so that I will know which way I should go. Let Your Word renew my mind so that I will not follow after the pattern of this world but after You. Lead me along paths of righteousness. Order my steps in Your Word. In all my dealings today let Your light shine through me. In the name of Jesus, amen.

Get Involved in Your Own Destiny

Behold, I will bring [Israel] health and healing; I will heal them and reveal to them the abundance of peace and truth.
—Jeremiah 33:6

Sometimes your success, progress, or blessings can be held up and hindered not because you are speaking negatively but because others have released negative words over your life and you have accepted them as true. Refuse to sit back and passively let life happen to you. Get actively involved in your own destiny. Aggressively reverse ill-spoken words, hexes, spells, and bad wishes. Proactively design, construct, and engineer your life. What do you want your life to look like next week, next year, or even at your funeral? Will you be remembered for your accomplishments—or only for what you might have done?

I am here by Your design and am specially equipped to complete a specific assignment. I am not inferior. I reject every word spoken over my life that is not in line with Your truth. According to Isaiah 53:5, by Your stripes I am healed from every physical and emotional wound. I reject all shame and condemnation. I declare their power broken off my life. I walk in the abundance of peace and truth from this day forward. In Jesus's name, amen.

May 11

God Already Knows

"For I know the plans I have for you," says the Lord. *"They are plans for good and not for disaster, to give you a future and a hope."*
—Jeremiah 29:11, nlt

God does not start a thing without knowing the outcome—He begins every work with the end in mind. Since He already knows the end from the beginning, He must know everything in between. Seek His face in prayer. Make inquiries concerning the plans He has for you. Discover His will as He speaks to your heart and mind, and then legislate His will in the earthly realm through daily declarations. By your words you establish life or death, blessings or curses, success or failure.

Father, You have known my end from the beginning, and You know everything in between. Teach me and instruct me in the way I should go. I commit to cooperate fully with Your purpose and plan. I declare that the best of my todays will become the worst of my tomorrows. I am empowered to accomplish the things I was born to do. You supply all my needs, and You prosper the works of my hands as I surrender completely to Your will. In the name of Jesus, amen.

Do You Know God's Voice?

The Spirit searches all things, yes, the deep things of God.
—1 Corinthians 2:10

The prayer warriors God is calling from this generation are men and women who know God's voice. They are so practiced in prayer that they can fall into deep intercession in an instant. They pray righteous prayers of desperate honesty that go straight to the heart of God. It is not that they get answers because of how much they speak, but rather because God is used to having them in the throne room and knows they are there for more than His promises.

Father, I come boldly before You, knowing that You will answer when I call and You will show me things I have not known. Your ears are open to my prayers. I decree and declare that this day is pregnant with Your purpose. I call forth strategic encounters, wonderful surprises, and supernatural breakthroughs. Cause my will to work in perfect harmony with Yours in Jesus's name, amen.

May 13

Your Miracle Already Exists

I set my heart to seek and search out by wisdom concerning all that is done under heaven; this burdensome task God has given to the sons of man, by which they may be exercised.
—Ecclesiastes 1:13

Man was created in the image of God and after His likeness. He was then given a mandate to rule and to dominate his world. He was given the delegated authority to preside over the earth and to protect it from negative forces that could create disequilibrium, distress, destitution, and disease. God said in the Book of Job that you shall decree a thing and it shall be established (Job 22:28). Your miracle already exists in the unseen "secret" realm. All secret things belong to God, but those things that are revealed belong to man. In Proverbs 25:2 (NLT) we read, "It is God's privilege to conceal things and the king's privilege to discover them." It is at the point of revelation—or divine inspiration—that God speaks to us all.

I decree and declare that everything this season should bring to me shall come forth. Spiritual, relational, political, and economic mountains must move. I break through walls and barricades that had been impenetrable. I advance past stubborn problems and inflexible people into new realms of miraculous provision, supernatural increase, influence, and favor. In the name of Jesus, amen.

Open Your Mind

He opens the ears of men, and seals their instruction.
—Job 33:16

God knows the end from the beginning and everything in between. And these are the things He wants to reveal to you. This is what God does: He opens up your mind and speaks inspirational thoughts so He can keep you from pursuing your own limited way. God's thoughts are of abundance and not lack—He wants you to live large and to bring you into a good life. He gives you divine, inspirational thoughts and the ability to speak them into existence so you will grow to fulfill His best plan for your life. He wants you to mature in wisdom, authority, and supernatural ability so you can bear witness to the splendor of His kingdom. Your miracle is already in existence, but it is up to you to learn to see it and to call it out.

Father, clear the "log jams" in my mind so Your Spirit will have unhindered access. Download Your creativity, wisdom, and supernatural strategy. I decree and declare that I will carry the promises of God full-term. I will not abort. I will possess my inheritance. The plans and purposes of God for my life shall prevail. In the name of Jesus, amen.

May 15

Perceive With Your Spiritual Sight

[Physical] eye has not seen, nor [physical] ear heard, nor have entered into the heart [understanding] of man the things which God has prepared for those who love Him.
—1 Corinthians 2:9

When we come to God in prayer, it is not only a time to lay our concerns and requests before God, but it is also a time for us to close our physical eyes and seek to perceive with our spiritual ones. It is time for us to open our spiritual ears and listen for the Holy Spirit to speak to us. Often we mistake Him for our own thoughts, and sometimes we mistake our own thoughts for the Holy Spirit speaking, but with practice, just as infants learn to distinguish their mother's voice from all the others in their world, so we learn to know the voice of the Good Shepherd. Such things must be perceived spiritually, and such spiritual attunement to the things of God comes through prayer.

Father, anoint my ears to hear Your voice with clarity and my eyes to see things as You see them. I refuse to be held back by limiting beliefs and small thinking. Cleanse my mind with the water of Your Word so I can become attuned to Your will. I know You desire to speak to me. Sharpen my discernment so I can receive from You without hindrance. In Jesus's name, amen.

What Have You Called Toward You?

I will give you the keys of the kingdom of heaven, and whatever you bind on earth will be bound in heaven, and whatever you loose on earth will be loosed in heaven.
—Matthew 16:19

A situation or circumstance generally comes because you have called it to you—you have given it permission to exist in your life. Casual words that on the surface may feel as though they are spoken out of humility—as though they are politely self-deprecating, politically correct, or not overly optimistic—can do more harm than you think. Remember, whatever you bind or loose on the earth will be bound or loosed in heaven.

Father, in the name of Jesus I close every door that has been opened to the enemy, whether knowingly or unknowingly. Any word spoken that is contrary to Your will for me, I bind now in the name of Jesus. I break patterns of insecurity and inferiority. I break the power of false humility that would have me settle for anything less than Your will for my life. Father, set a watch over my mouth and keep the door of my lips. Let no corrupt communication proceed from me. In the name of Jesus, amen.

May 17

Know That It Is God

Beloved, do not believe every spirit, but test the spirits to see whether they are from God.
—1 John 4:1, esv

Spiritual perceptions can seem so strange and make us very uncomfortable. The people struggling to understand them can make mistakes in their interpretations, and for many people this makes them doubt their sincerity. They think these people are making things up to get attention rather than struggling to understand the glimpses God has given them of His perspective. Of course, this gives good reason not to be quick to proclaim what God is showing you in prayer until you are sure you understand it and that it is truly from God. But this does not justify the temptation of going about with your spiritual eyes closed simply because it is easier.

Father, open the eyes of my understanding. I want to know Your will. Download divine insights and revelation, creative ideas, and cutting-edge concepts. Send angels to frustrate anything that would seek to derail Your plans and purposes for me. I renounce all doubt and unbelief that would prevent me from trusting the prophetic words and visions You give me. Father, open my eyes and ears to the things of the Spirit. I want all You have for me. In Jesus's name, amen.

God's Reward Is for You

It's impossible to please God apart from faith. And why? Because anyone who wants to approach God must believe both that he exists and that he cares enough to respond to those who seek him.

—Hebrews 11:6, The Message

There should be no doubt in your mind that God wants to bless and prosper you. He wants you to succeed and not fail. He wants the very best for you. Remember, those who come to God must believe that He rewards those who diligently seek Him. This is because the one thing that pleases God is your faith.

Father, I believe You want what's best for me. I know Your plans for me are good; they are plans to prosper me and not to harm me, plans to give me hope and a future. I choose to walk by faith and not by sight. I follow Your ways and believe that You will prosper the works of my hands. You have given me everything I need for life and godliness. I know that if I just believe, nothing shall be impossible for me. I reject all doubt and unbelief so that I may move from glory to glory and from faith to faith. In Jesus's name, amen.

May 19

You Can Overcome It

Now salvation, and strength, and the kingdom of our God, and the power of His Christ have come, for the accuser of our brethren, who accused them before our God day and night, has been cast down. And they overcame him by the blood of the Lamb and by the word of their testimony.
—Revelation 12:10–11

Let your declarations be informed by the following revolutionary—and "revelationary"—truth: Your enemy is overcome by the blood of the Lamb and the word of your testimony. You must declare, "He who is in [me] is greater than he who is in the world" (1 John 4:4), and, "In all these things we are more than conquerors through Him who loved us" (Rom. 8:37). Believe and confess. Speak with conviction and confess with expectation. Expect that whatever you are decreeing will come to pass.

I am more than a conqueror through Him who loves us. He who is in me is greater than he who is in the world. I stand in faith declaring that all of Your promises are yes and amen in You. Every mountain standing in the way of Your promises must be removed and cast into sea. Every mountain of oppression or depression, lack and frustration, dysfunction and chaos must go in the name of Jesus. I declare these things done in the name of Jesus. Amen.

May 20

Sealed in the Spirit Realm

You will also declare a thing, and it will be established for you; so light will shine on your ways.
—Job 22:28

Since the spirit realm is the causal realm, expect that whatever you are praying will manifest on this side of glory because it has already been sealed in the spirit realm. God has already released every possibility before the foundation of the world. Do not be counterproductive in your declarations by decreeing one thing and confessing the other. Be consistent in knowing that when you commit to the releasing of those things that pertain to your life, God is saying that whatsoever (positive or negative, faith or unbelief) you loose is loosed, and whatsoever you bind is bound. Remember, as soon as a declaration leaves your mouth, it has already happened.

Father, I decree and declare that my mouth is the pen of a ready writer. I proclaim Your Word and not my own will. I press past the boundary lines the enemy has drawn, and I take every area that has been purposed for me. The enemy is defeated, and his efforts to derail my destiny will not prosper. I decree and declare that the plans of God will prevail in my life. In Jesus's name, amen.

May 21

Accomplish God's Will

I tell you the truth, my Father will give you whatever you ask in my name.
—John 16:23, NIV

God delegated authority to you, as a believer, that you may accomplish His will on the earth. Inherent within this divine authority is the mantle of responsibility and accountability. You are responsible to speak in accordance with the divine will that has been spoken concerning you. Kingdom authority demands that you become proactive in the establishment of purpose in your life experience. You are not to be dominated by circumstances—you are to take authority over them and decree the will of God into manifestation in the name of Jesus.

Father, I will not let circumstances dictate my future. I declare Your will over my life and my day: I walk in the peace of God. My family is blessed and my workplace is in order. I have the mind of Christ; therefore my thoughts are filled with creative and inventive ideas that advance Your kingdom. My bank accounts have sufficient resources to meet my needs and to help others. I give to You with a cheerful heart. You do all things well, and You have deposited the same spirit of excellence in me. Bless the works of my hands and let Your favor rest on me today. In Jesus's name, amen.

Practice Prayer-Walking

[Jabez] was the one who prayed to the God of Israel: "Oh, that you would bless me and expand my territory! Please be with me in all that I do, and keep me from all trouble and pain!" And God granted him his request.
—1 Chronicles 4:10, NLT

Develop the habit of prayer-walking. As you walk, think about God's promise to enlarge your territory and give you every place you set your foot. As you walk, declare God's Word and watch what God will do. He is getting ready to blow your mind with blessings. He will reverse negative circumstances. He will position you for supernatural abundance and unprecedented favor. Without a shadow of doubt, He will show up mighty on your behalf. Your breakthrough and miracles are on the way!

Father, I claim new territory for Your kingdom. I take new intellectual territory; I declare that my mind is filled with deeper revelation of Your truth. I take new spiritual territory; I declare that all delays, setbacks, and holdups are destroyed in the name of Jesus. I claim new professional territory; my gifts make room for me and usher me into the presence of the great. I effect change in the world through prayer. I declare a shift in the atmosphere in my home, workplace, church, and ministry. I walk boldly in the authority I have in You. In Jesus's name, amen.

May 23

Walk in the Spirit

Since we live by the Spirit, let us keep in step with the Spirit.
—Galatians 5:25, niv

I have personally integrated declarations into my daily exercise routine. I need to exercise to maintain my health, and I love to walk, so I accomplish two life-sustaining essentials with one activity. This practice not only promotes physical strength, stamina, and overall health, but it also builds strong prayer muscles, increasing spiritual stamina and fortitude. Think about "walking in the Spirit" as you walk out your destiny with your words. Practice keeping step with the Spirit as you declare His promises over your life.

Father, I belong to You, and I crucify my flesh with its passions and lusts. I embody the fruit of the Spirit. Because I walk with You, I don't gratify the lusts of the flesh. I remain strong in my faith. I know that blessing comes to those who heed Your voice, so I put my trust in You and obey Your Word. Your commandments are good. Your statutes are right. They give life, and I do not grow weary in doing well for I know that in due season I shall reap, because I will not faint. Amen.

May 24

Get a New Set of Keys

For as he [a man or woman] thinks in his heart, so is he.
—Proverbs 23:7

Many people have come to believe life is a mystery that cannot be solved. They think success and prosperity are destined for everyone except them, and they feel powerless and victimized as the events of their lives spiral out of control. They would do something about it if they knew what to do, but they've tried everything they know and have come up empty every time. What they need is a new set of keys to unlock all God is holding for them in their lives. The truth is, we define our lives by our every thought and word. If we want our lives to change, it all starts with what we think and say.

I can hide nothing from You, Father. You know my ways and what is truly in my heart. Weed out everything in me that is not like You. Let my words reflect Your Word, my heart reflect Your heart, and my thoughts reflect Your thoughts. I submit to Your complete control. I decree and declare that as I renew my mind with Your Word, everything about me is changing for my good and Your glory in the name of Jesus. Amen.

May 25

Live Without Lack

I pray that you may be active in sharing your faith, so that you will have a full understanding of every good thing we have in Christ.
—Philemon 6, NIV

When I say "abundance," I am not talking about materialism or consumerism. What I am talking about is the fact that it is God's will for you to live without lack—to provide you with every possible thing you need to successfully fulfill your purpose and maximize your potential. This certainly includes material things, but more importantly it means Spirit-inspired thoughts, declarations, and conversations; divinely appointed relationships, business opportunities, and challenges; and above all else, supernatural gifts and abilities as you acknowledge every good thing that is in you in Christ.

Father, thank You for giving me everything I need for life and godliness. You have given me all I need to fulfill Your plan. I am complete in You and lacking nothing. I will not listen to the enemy's attempts to make me feel inferior or inadequate. Faithful is He who called me who also will do it. You not only called me, but also You have qualified me to accomplish my assignment in the earth. I will not doubt Your faithfulness to complete the good work You have begun in me. In Jesus's name, amen.

Don't Be Double-Minded

A double-minded man [is] unstable in all his ways.
—James 1:8

A double-minded person is a person with conflicting thoughts—someone who holds two different opinions at the same time. That person is the pilot who steers his ship toward one port for a while, then reverses to steer it toward another in the opposite direction. He is like "a wave of the sea driven and tossed by the wind" (v. 6). At one point your life is headed toward blessings because that is what you have spoken, and the next it is headed toward cursing because that is now what your mouth is proclaiming.

Father, I will not be like a wave of the sea, tossed to and fro by every circumstance that comes my way. I will trust You and not doubt because the one who doubts should not expect to receive anything from You. I expect to receive from You because I stand in faith, knowing the Word I proclaim over my life will not return void. I decree and declare that my name will not be associated with indecisiveness or confusion. I am stable emotionally, financially, and spiritually. When I don't know what to do, I ask You, and You give me wisdom generously. Father, redeem any time I may have lost, and let me move boldly into my destiny. In the name of Jesus, amen.

May 27

Glimpse the Spiritual Superhighway

And he dreamed: A stairway was set on the ground and it reached all the way to the sky; angels of God were going up and going down on it.
—Genesis 28:12, The Message

Throughout the Bible we learn that God cannot intervene on the earth unless someone gives permission for the answer to exist in the material world. Answers are held up in the heavenlies and locked up in the realm of the spirit until there is a person able to pick up on the correct frequency and act as a conduit to release God's will into the earth. This is illustrated by Jacob's experience in the Book of Genesis. Jacob was able to get a glimpse of a spiritual superhighway. I believe these superhighways are our thoughts. This is where we pick up inspiration. These inspirational thoughts seem to appear out of thin air, but really they are circulating in the realm of the spirit.

Father, in the name of Jesus I declare that my prayers have free passage to ascend into the realm of the supernatural. They will not be earthbound. I come into agreement with heaven, and I proclaim Your truth. Your anointing breaks every yoke. Let there be a breakthrough in the heavens and release everything that is assigned to me. In Jesus's name, amen.

Use a Variety of Strategies

He said to them, Therefore every teacher and interpreter of the Sacred Writings who has been instructed about and trained for the kingdom of heaven and has become a disciple is like a householder who brings forth out of his storehouse treasure that is new and [treasure that is] old [the fresh as well as the familiar].

—Matthew 13:52, amp

Jesus states that a person who is coached to participate in the kingdom of heaven is one who is able to tap into both ancient truth and fresh wisdom. In other words, we seek insight and guidance for prayer from both the Old and the New Testaments. To keep your prayer life vibrant and exciting, you should use a variety of strategies as well as a diversity of goals.

Father, as I seek fresh strategies to make this day more productive, let me never forget the wisdom of the aged. As I seek new revelation, let me never forget the foundational truths of Scripture. Cause me to discern which strategy is needed at the time. In the name of Jesus, amen.

May 29

Shift the Atmosphere

Sheer muscle and willpower don't make anything happen. Every word I've spoken to you is a Spirit-word, and so it is life-making.
—John 6:63, The Message

In a very real sense our words can shift the atmosphere around us. That is the power of intercessory prayer—and when we begin to speak in our daily lives the things that we pray in private, change happens. We need to realize that in a very tangible way, our words—*all of our words taken as a whole*—shape our realities.

In the name of Jesus I declare that this is a season of breakthrough. I command the atmosphere to shift. Spiritual climate—shift in the name of Jesus. Economic climate—shift in the name of Jesus. I decree and declare that the conditions are right for my home, my ministry, and my workplace to thrive. I declare that every bit of lukewarmness in me is being replaced by the fire of God. I am being changed and becoming more like Christ. Father, make me more like You. Your kingdom is my priority and Your will is my desire. In the name of Jesus, amen.

May 30

Surrender Yourself to God's Word

If you abide in Me, and My words abide in you, you will ask what you desire, and it shall be done for you. By this My Father is glorified, that you bear much fruit; so you will be My disciples.
—John 15:7–8

We need to be careful not to speak what we want to see happen without truly surrendering ourselves to what is written in Scripture. This would make us unable to combine what we are saying with genuine faith. It requires us to invest more time studying God's Word so more of His truth might be expressed in what we are saying. We cannot speak one way in prayer and another way in our day-to-day life, or else our casual doubt, negativity, and unbelief won't affect what we are trying to stand in faith to see happen. This is not how God intended it.

Father, I submit to Your Word. If I obey You, all will be well. Jesus didn't speak on His own authority, and neither will I. I will declare Your Word. Your laws are perfect; Your commands are pure. They are to be desired more than gold because in keeping them there is great reward. Sanctify me with Your truth, and order my steps in Your Word. In Jesus's name, amen.

May 31

Be Perfect

If you could find someone whose speech was perfectly true, you'd have a perfect person, in perfect control of life.
—James 3:2, The Message

You may have some hang-ups about the word *perfect*. We have associated that word with brash arrogance, unattainable standards, or unreasonable expectations. But here in James the word means "complete" or "mature." In other words, someone who controls their tongue is a grown-up. They aren't ruled by the whims of childhood or adolescence. They don't throw temper tantrums on the floor. They are people with an aim and a purpose, focused on what is before them and aligning their words and their behaviors accordingly.

Father, when I was a child I spoke like a child. But now that I am grown, I put away childish things. I will not be distracted by what other people are saying and doing. I keep my eyes on You, because You know the way I should go. You designed my path, and I will follow it. According to 2 Timothy 3:17, I decree and declare that I am perfect in You and thoroughly equipped for every good work. In Jesus's name, amen.

June

June 1

Set Your Course

You're blessed when you stay on course, walking steadily on the road revealed by God. You're blessed when you follow his directions, doing your best to find him.... Oh, that my steps might be steady, keeping to the course you set; then I'd never have any regrets in comparing my life with your counsel.

—Psalm 119:1–6, The Message

Those who set their course follow in the counsel of God—and this doesn't make them stiff or humorless, either. It makes them intentional. They enjoy life. They enjoy their work. They enjoy their family. They enjoy their church. They are the type of people who are going somewhere. They happen to life; life doesn't just happen to them. These are the type of people who don't throw out words as if they are some magical incantation that will bring them what they want. They use what they say to set their course.

Father, I stand in Your counsel. I do not go off on my own. I follow the path You set. You order my steps in Your Word. You lead me by the hand. Because I trust and obey Your Word, my way shall be prosperous and I will eat the good of the land. In the name of Jesus, amen.

June 2

The Power of the Tongue

The tongue is so set among our members that it defiles the whole body, and sets on fire the course of nature.
—James 3:6

James warns us that the power of the tongue can too easily be used in the wrong way. He also warns that we should be "swift to hear, slow to speak, slow to wrath" (James 1:19). Since the tongue is so potent, we should never speak rashly or in anger. Why? Because what we say matters. What we say either edifies or poisons reality.

Out of the abundance of the heart the mouth speaks, so, Father, create in me a clean heart, and renew a right spirit in me. Let my life reflect the fruit of the Spirit and not the weaknesses of my temperament or the proclivity of my flesh. Let the words of my mouth and the meditations of my heart be acceptable in Your sight. Lord, You are my strength and my redeemer. Let no corrupt communication proceed out of my mouth. You have put the power of life and death within my mouth, and I will use my tongue to proclaim Your Word. According to Romans 10:8, I decree and declare that Your Word is in my mouth and my heart. Because of You, the words I speak are spirit and life. In Jesus's name, amen.

June 3

Your Words Control Your Direction

A word out of your mouth may seem of no account, but it can accomplish nearly anything—or destroy it!
—James 3:5, The Message

Saying what we want—finding the Bible promises that support our desires or what we are interceding for and repeating them over and over—is relatively easy. Anyone can do that. And while that is a good thing to do, it is just the beginning. If you pull the bridle in one direction but the rest of the horse does not go in that direction, what good is the bit? If you turn the rudder but the ship's course stays the same, what good is trying to steer? No, it is only when the rest of our being turns to follow where we are directing by using the bit or the rudder that we actually change our lives or the lives of others through our prayers. Notice that the winds of life still blow, but when we use our tongue as the rudder of our actions and attitudes, the winds don't control where we are going; our words do.

Let Your Word renew my mind and transform the way I live. I do not only hear the Word; I also do what it says. Blessings overtake me because I heed Your voice. Guide me continually in Your truth; teach me, for You are the God of my salvation. In Jesus's name, amen.

Don't Contradict Your Faith

Does a spring send forth fresh water and bitter from the same opening? Can a fig tree, my brethren, bear olives, or a grapevine bear figs?
—James 3:11–12

When we start to steer our lives by our words, we are slower to speak because we weigh everything that comes out of our mouths more conscientiously. We want to say things that truly represent what we mean and steer us in the right direction. We avoid speaking words that contradict our faith or our prayers. We don't belittle others or spit venom at them with the same mouths we use to praise God.

Father, I know my tongue is powerful. With my mouth I can choose to speak blessings or curses. I do not speak carelessly. I do not rely on earthly wisdom. I do not speak out of jealously or selfish ambition, because that produces disorder. Rather, I love my enemies, and I refuse to repay evil with evil. Father, fill my heart with the wisdom from above—which is pure, peaceable, open to reason, and full of mercy and good fruit—so that my speech sows peace and I reap a harvest of righteousness. In the name of Jesus, amen.

June 5

Align With Your Words

Whatever you do in word or deed, do all in the name of the Lord Jesus.
—Colossians 3:17

Our actions and attitudes need to align with the direction our words are plotting out. We become "perfect" in word and deed as both line up to accomplish what we have been put on the earth to do. We become "integrous" at the most fundamental meaning of the word—there is a 100 percent alignment between who we are on the inside and who we are on the outside. Like steel or another alloy with high integrity, we are pure in motive and action through and through—and from that comes great strength.

Father, I do not honor You with my words only, but I also honor You with my deeds. Because I walk in integrity, I will inhabit the land You have reserved for me, and I will remain in it. My lips will not speak falsehood; my tongue will not utter deceit. I declare that my children are blessed because I walk uprightly. I will be delivered in times of trouble. I will not subject the Word of God to reproach by failing to follow Your ways. I walk uprightly, with sound speech, so that no one has anything evil to say of me. In Jesus's name, amen.

June 6

USE YOUR WORDS WISELY

There is one whose rash words are like sword thrusts, but the tongue of the wise brings healing.
—PROVERBS 12:18, ESV

Words are a spiritual force. They are containers shaped by our thoughts, intentions, and meaning—tools that chisel our lives and the lives of those around us into masterpieces. However, a sculptor who doesn't understand his tools, their purposes, and how to use them will not create anything worthy of display. Therefore, we must study language and the Word of God to be able to pick the right word for the right occasion. We must both control and understand what is coming out of our mouths. You don't use a mallet to smooth edges, and you can't refine detail with a jackhammer. It is the same whether we speak to God or to human beings. The words we choose in public or in our prayer closets matter more than you'd think.

Father, let my speech be always gracious, seasoned with salt, that it may minister to the hearers. I will not be hasty with my words You have given me wisdom; therefore, I restrain my words and use my mouth to commend knowledge. I choose to bridle my tongue, so that my faith before You may be pure and undefiled. In Jesus's name, amen.

June 7

Prayer Helps You See

He shall be like a tree planted by the rivers of water, that brings forth its fruit in its season, whose leaf also shall not wither; and whatever he does shall prosper.

—Psalm 1:3

Prayer changes your perception and gives you the ability to see things from God's perspective. It is as if a fog that you never noticed before begins to lift. As you face situations and decisions, wisdom begins to show you more clearly the right way to go. Revelation about the specific actions you need to take is there when you need it. The words for any certain circumstance just well up within you when you need to speak them. It's not that some incredible manifestation happens. It's just that whatever you do or say prospers because of prayer. Like the tree planted by a stream, your spiritual roots tap into a fresh supply of power, which is available upon demand.

I decree and declare that I handle each day You give me with prayer. Because I bring my needs to You, I am not anxious for anything, but Your peace guards my heart and mind. I turn to You, and You give me wisdom; I seek Your instruction, and You show me the way I should go. I don't worry about the future because You keep my footing sure. Thank You, Lord, for leading me by the hand. Amen.

Prayer Is Not Manipulation

Here's what I want you to do: Find a quiet, secluded place so you won't be tempted to role-play before God. Just be there as simply and honestly as you can manage. The focus will shift from you to God, and you will begin to sense his grace.
—Matthew 6:6, The Message

Prayers work wonders or can create blunders if we don't understand the power of the spoken word. We are not trying to talk God into doing things He knows are bad ideas or that were birthed out of selfishness. Prayer is not manipulation—and neither should our speech be. When we go to God in prayer, we are reminding Him of His nature with praise, celebrating His promises with our petitions, and embracing His love as we speak on behalf of others. We are not twisting things so that we can get our own way. We are partnering with Him in seeing His kingdom manifest.

Father, I will not twist Your Word to get my own way. I listen for Your direction and partner with what You're doing. My desire is to do Your will, not my own. I release You to move in my heart. Give me the desires You want me to have so I honor You with everything I do and with every prayer I lift up to You today. In the name of Jesus, amen.

June 9

Keep in Line With Your Prayers

Don't pick on people, jump on their failures, criticize their faults—unless, of course, you want the same treatment. That critical spirit has a way of boomeranging....It's this whole traveling road-show mentality all over again, playing a holier-than-thou part instead of just living your part.
—Matthew 7:1–5, The Message

When we "leave" prayer and go out into the world, we don't contradict the faith we expressed in prayer with doubt expressed to others. This is one expression of "praying without ceasing"—what we say to others throughout the day is in line with what we spoke to God about in private. And then our actions and attitudes follow suit. Our whole being focuses in on our goals and purposes with laser-like precision. Not only that, but we also begin to affect the atmosphere wherever we go. It is like we walk around in an ever-enlarging cloud of the kingdom of God, and the more places we go and the more consistent we are in aligning our words and actions with the Word and will of God, the bigger that cloud grows around us and over those we interact with each day.

My words determine the course of my entire day. So I will not only pray Your Word today, but I will also keep declaring and believing it, knowing You will answer because I pray according to Your will. In the name of Jesus, amen.

Time for a Paradigm Shift

Therefore, my beloved brothers, be steadfast, immovable, always abounding in the work of the Lord, knowing that in the Lord your labor is not in vain.
—1 Corinthians 15:58, esv

To see permanent change, you must have a permanent paradigm shift. You don't create a path through a forest by taking a new route each time to cross it. You have to be consistent in your words, prayers, and actions. As we are focused and intentional in thought and speech, we permanently alter our perceptions and our habits, and thus align our actions with what we are believing for in prayer, creating a lifestyle of godliness and power.

Father, I will remain steadfast and immovable in You, holding on to Your promises and always trusting in Your Word. I know my efforts are not in vain. I abide in Your Word, and its truth sets me free. I decree and declare that my words are filled with righteousness; there is nothing crooked or perverse in them. You awaken me every morning and open my ears to receive Your instructions. I learn from You and do not rebel. You give me a wise and discerning mind, and I will act in accordance with Your Word. In Jesus's name, amen.

June 11

Create a New Reality

God...gives life to the dead and calls into being that which does not exist.
—Romans 4:17, nas

You are, literally, creating reality by your prayers and your words. You are doing it every day with the thoughts you are thinking, the words you are speaking, and the prayers that, as a result, you are praying. While it remains true that the key to seeing everything is to first believe it, there is, in fact, scientific evidence to support the concept that your words shape your own world. Seeing does not always produce believing, but believing will produce seeing.

Father, I commit to honor You with my words and actions today. I decree and declare that I will lay hold of the things You have prepared for me. There will be no holdups, setbacks, or delays. You are moving me toward Your perfect plan for me, no matter what things look like in the natural realm. I am not moved by circumstances. I walk by faith and not sight. I will keep on believing until Your will manifests in my life. In the name of Jesus, amen.

June 12

Speak It Into Being

By faith we understand that the worlds were framed by the word of God, so that the things which are seen were not made of things which are visible.
—Hebrews 11:3

Your expectations, thoughts, and beliefs manifest in your speech and change the things around you. Though it is to a lesser degree, it is the same principle by which God spoke the world into being in Genesis 1. He formed ideas of what He wanted, infused those meanings into words, spoke them into the nothingness, and the universe we live in today was formed.

Father, You spoke into nothingness and created the world. I speak into this day and declare that it will cooperate with Your plans. Anything sent to frustrate Your purposes for this day is bound now in the name of Jesus and rendered ineffective. I declare that today is pregnant with destiny. Thank You, Father, for divine connections that advance Your kingdom. Lord, give me wisdom and understanding to be more efficient in my work; open doors to new opportunities and new revelation in the name of Jesus. Father, bless the works of my hands; I choose to glorify You in all I do. In the name of Jesus, amen.

June 13

Intercession Creates New Realities

The effective, fervent prayer of a righteous man avails much.
—James 5:16

All matter that you see in this physical dimension is simply energy vibrating in such a way that it takes on static properties. When it does this, you perceive things as being solid. Matter is, however, totally unsubstantial. Nearly 99 percent of an atom (which makes up all the matter there is) is actually "empty space." That means that through our positive confessions of faith or expectations, we can influence how the world around us takes form. Prayer, in essence, is our opportunity to speak the language of change. As you pray and decree a thing, the meaning, purpose, and faith invested in your words travel at a frequency affecting anything and everything that flows along its path at a subatomic level. In this light thoughts are, in fact, things. Thoughts are given vitality by your belief, attitudes, and emotions. They are activated by the law of focused attention.

Father, I delight in Your Word; I mediate on it day and night, and You make my way prosperous. I cancel the effect of negative, self-defeating thoughts now in the name of Jesus. I have a fresh mind and fresh excitement. I have great anticipation of the good things You will do today. In Jesus's name, amen.

June 14

WHAT'S YOUR FOCUS?

The words that I speak to you are spirit, and they are life.
—JOHN 6:63

Whatever you give your consideration to—whatever you focus on—grows in terms of relevance, importance, and significance. Words, whether positive or negative, are a powerful, driving force. In order to express itself, your faith must attach itself to an image formed by your words so that the outward manifestation has a pattern after which to form.

Father, I declare that my thoughts are governed only by "things true, noble, reputable, authentic, compelling, gracious—the best, not the worst; the beautiful, not the ugly; things to praise, not things to curse" (Phil. 4:8–9, THE MESSAGE). I keep Your words on my lips, and I press toward my purpose and calling. I look to You, the author and finisher of my faith, and I keep my focus on the goal You set before me. Bringing Your kingdom is my priority. I follow hard after You. Let Your will be done in and through me. In Jesus's name, amen.

June 15

God Will Share His Plans

And the prayer of faith will save the sick, and the Lord will raise him up. And if he has committed sins, he will be forgiven.
—James 5:15

God knows the end from the beginning, and if we will spend time in prayer listening for His guidance, He will share it with us. His plans and purposes for the earth can come to pass only through those with legal jurisdiction on our planet. We are the key. But it takes faith. You must develop the courage and faith to take the risk to pull away, pray, and then sit quietly and wait for God to answer. This is how we operate in the realm of faith. This is how we bring our thoughts, ideas, dreams, and visions to pass.

Father, I am not too busy to pull away and seek You. I give You the firstfruits of my day. When I seek You, I find You, for You long to reveal Yourself to me. As I press in to You, give me a word for each situation. I wait patiently for Your word. "I would have lost heart, unless I had believed that I would see the goodness of the Lord in the land of the living" (Ps. 27:13). But I wait for You, and You renew my strength. I know that You are my help and shield, and my salvation comes from You. In Jesus's name, amen.

Give Freedom, Not Manipulation

Be generous with your lives. By opening up to others, you'll prompt people to open up with God, this generous Father in heaven.
—Matthew 5:16, The Message

As we pray for others and speak out God's Word over our atmospheres, we need to remember that just as God respects the jurisdiction each of us has over our own lives and choices, we must have the same respect for those we are praying for. We should be praying that God opens their eyes so that they can see the truth and make the right choices for themselves (just as God does for each of us who call on His name), not that God will make those we are praying for do this or that. After all, Jesus has already done everything He needs to do to see that a person is saved, but He left it to each of us to decide on our own to accept His free gift of salvation or not. In His great love He will not even force heaven upon any of us.

Father, in the name of Jesus I come against all forms of manipulation today. I cancel the assignment of those who would seek to manipulate me into following their will over Yours, and I repent for any times I have tried to force my will on others. I commit my plans to You and put my desires in Your capable hands. In Jesus's name, amen.

June 17

Turn On the Light

You ask and do not receive, because you ask wrongly, to spend it on your passions.
—James 4:3, esv

This is not some kind of magical thinking. Speaking scriptures out over our situations is not like something out of the Harry Potter series. We are not manipulating people, atmospheres, or events to get what we want; we are speaking out God's will over them, and His laws and promises to enforce that will. Once again intercession is not manipulation; it is turning on the light so those stumbling in the dark can finally find their ways to the door for themselves. Remember, Esther didn't just petition that the Jews would be saved—she requested they be armed and equipped to fend for themselves.

Father, guide me with Your Word as I pray. Do not let me speak of myself. It is Your Word that will change minds and hearts, so I commit to declare Your Word over my life and others' lives. You desire that everyone be saved and come into the knowledge of the truth. Let Your will be done. Father, cause Your light to shine through me so others can find their way. In Jesus's name, amen.

Exercise Your Mind

God's Word is an indispensable weapon. In the same way, prayer is essential in this ongoing warfare. Pray hard and long. Pray for your brothers and sisters. Keep your eyes open. Keep each other's spirits up so that no one falls behind or drops out.

—Ephesians 6:17–18, The Message

Intercession takes mental strength and spiritual fortitude, which are developed in the same way your natural strength is. You must "exercise" regularly. You must meditate on the meaning of your and God's words night and day. Your mind-set and beliefs must align with your words and behaviors. To take your thoughts to the next level—to the creation of witty ideas and innovative inventions—practice thinking in terms of possibilities. Believe the best and speak according to those beliefs until it becomes a habit. When you believe you can influence the world through prayer—when you are able to open your mind to the miraculous and expect better outcomes—then you will begin to see change come to pass. This will drive your work, and God will show you answers and bless the things you set your hands to do.

I decree and declare that the Spirit of the living God has precedence over my mind. Because the mind of Christ rules and reign over my mind, body, and spirit, I have heavenly ambitions and the discipline to see them cultivated and carried through to completion. In the name of Jesus, amen.

June 19

We Want a Taste of Infinity

God can do anything, you know—far more than you could ever imagine or guess or request in your wildest dreams! He does it by not pushing us around but by working within us, his Spirit deeply and gently within us.
—Ephesians 3:20, The Message

Today we stand as heirs of promises beyond our wildest hopes and imaginings, but we are handicapped by being born into the constraints of this world with ears untrained to hear the pulse of heaven. We grow up thinking everything that exists is defined by what we experience with our physical senses. Our minds are framed by it, even as the eternity in our hearts cries out for more—for a taste of the infinite. Why do you think stories about magic, superheroes, and miracles are so popular today? We know in our deepest selves that there is a world more real out there than the one we live in, but, confused by the world's lies, too many of us settle for simple stories rather than taking on the quest of knowing the one true God—the only real answer to the call of eternity in our hearts.

Father, cause me to experience You on a deeper level. I open my mind and heart to the supernatural. Awaken within me a spirit of expectation. Give me dreams, visions, and divine encounters. I long to know You more. In the name of Jesus, amen.

June 20

Tap Into the Conversation

He chose us in Him before the foundation of the world, that we should be holy and without blame before Him in love.
—Ephesians 1:4

There's a conversation that has been going on from long before this universe was even created—a conversation taking place in the spiritual realm in the throne room of heaven. Before the fall of humanity Adam and Eve were part of it, and there is something buried in each of our hearts that tells us we were created to be part of it as well. It's a dialogue built into the very fabric of our DNA. We long for it. We yearn to be in on it.

Father, it is my privilege to come boldly into Your presence today. In Your presence I have fullness of joy. In Your presence I am refreshed and renewed. I desire to walk and talk with You as You walked and talked with Adam and Eve in the garden. Let me be in sync and in season with Your original plan and purpose. Give me prophetic revelation so that my prayers are like strategic missiles that reach their targets and accomplish the divine purposes for which they have been sent. In Your presence my life is laid bare. Search me, oh, God, and see if there is any unrighteous way in me. Let Your fire fill my heart. In Jesus's name, amen.

June 21

Do Battle in the Trenches

If you have run with the footmen, and they have wearied you, then how can you contend with horses?
—Jeremiah 12:5

Before you can be a privileged confidante and adviser fully participating in the big conversation of heaven, you must first learn to do battle in the trenches of your own personal life and the world it touches. Before you can pray for the building of a five-thousand-seat church, you must first learn to successfully pray to cover your rent or mortgage. You will never know how to win your city for Jesus until you know how to pray your neighbors and your family into the kingdom. You will never hear the strategies of heaven for your nation until you know how to hear the plans and purposes of heaven for your own life.

Father, all I need is faith the size of a mustard seed. With that much faith I can tell mountains to move. So I stand in faith today, believing that You will meet every need and respond to every care. I bring everything that concerns me to You, knowing that nothing is too small. The same God who saved me can save my loved ones, and You can also change cities and nations. My faith is rising, even today, as I depend completely on You. In Jesus's name, amen.

June 22

Enter the Throne Room

Now it came to pass, as He was praying in a certain place, when He ceased, that one of His disciples said to Him, "Lord, teach us to pray, as John also taught his disciples."
—Luke 11:1

All of this starts with you, in your prayer closet, laying your heart and your requests before the throne of heaven *every day*. If you can't get a word from heaven for today, how do you expect to get the plan of heaven for this year? For your lifetime? For your city, your nation, or your world? How will you learn the things God wants you to know about who you are in His kingdom and what He has for you to do in it?

The veil has been torn, and I now have direct access to You, Lord. Give me Your wisdom. Reveal Your Word to me and download prophetic insight so I will know how I ought to pray. I bring my every need before You. I cast my cares on You, and I know You will sustain me. You will not let the righteous be forsaken. I am righteous, and I will not be forsaken. You are my refuge and strength, an ever-present help in trouble. I will not fear the future because I trust in You. In Jesus's name, amen.

June 23

Learn How to Pray

If you abide in Me, and My words abide in you, you will ask what you desire, and it shall be done for you. By this My Father is glorified, that you bear much fruit; so you will be My disciples.
—John 15:7–8

God doesn't promote privates into generals overnight because He knows the risks. Authority without discipline is harmful for both leaders and followers. How often have we seen men and women rise up too quickly in the body of Christ only to crash and burn because they ran things the way the world does rather than how they were instructed from heaven? We are all called into ministry—whether it is as businesspeople, teachers, doctors, lawyers, janitors, artists, legislators, or whatever else God has put on our hearts. While each calling takes a specific expertise and requires unique talents and gifts, they all have one thing in common: success is determined by one's ability to know how to pray and get direction from heaven.

Father, You gave me the gifts and abilities I have, but You know best how I should use them. You are the potter; I am the clay. Train my ear to hear Your voice. I accept the instructions from Your mouth, and I lay up Your words in my heart. Father, guide me in the way I should go and make my way prosperous. In the name of Jesus, amen.

Give God Everything You Have

Ask, and it will be given to you; seek, and you will find; knock, and it will be opened to you. For everyone who asks receives, and the one who seeks finds, and to the one who knocks it will be opened.
—Matthew 7:7–8, esv

Our Father is a good Father, and He wants you to have what you need. When you ask for one thing, He is not going to give you something that is of no use or might be harmful. But He's not a vending machine you can just pop a few coins into, get what you want, and then walk away from either. He wants a relationship with you. To have this, you must give Him what He wants—your heart. You must continue to knock and seek if you hope to find. You have to spend time sitting at His feet, letting Him teach and purify you. It is the only way you can cut through the static of your own mind in order to hear His answer.

Father, I love You will all my heart, my soul, and my mind. I hold nothing back from You. I release You to work in my life. Make me more like You! Make me a servant. I hunger and thirst after righteousness, and Your Word says I will be filled. Fill me with more of You, Lord. Let nothing in my life be the same. In Jesus's name, amen.

June 25

Have Patience and Faith

I say to you, though he will not rise [from bed] and give [bread] to him because he is his friend, yet because of his persistence he will rise and give him as many as he needs.
—Luke 11:8

Do you have faith like the impertinent neighbor in Luke 11:5–8? Will you go to the door of heaven and keep knocking until you get what you need? Do you believe that when you go and knock, you will hear an answer from the other side of the door? Because I'm telling you here and now, if you don't keep after it, if you're unsure you will get an answer, if you are hesitant or grow frustrated, you will never get what you are after. But if you have patience and faith in prayer, there is nothing in heaven our Father won't make available to you.

Father, I will not be quiet in prayer. I will keep on asking, keep on seeking, and keep on believing until there is breakthrough. I press in to You, and do not grow weary in well doing. In due season I will reap because I will not faint. I thank You in advance for the victory. In Jesus's name, amen.

June 26

Open Your Heart to the Eternal

When you pray, say: Our Father in heaven, hallowed be Your name. Your kingdom come. Your will be done on earth as it is in heaven.

—Luke 11:2

In the revolutionary prayer Jesus offered in Luke 11:2–4, He gave His disciples not only an outline of what to pray for daily—a starting place for consistently knocking on the door of heaven—but also the means of transforming their own minds from a world of doubt, oppression, and failure into a mind-set of heaven—one of faith, provision, and overcoming. He was not teaching them something to be repeated *ad nauseam* but a dynamic way to open hearts to the infinite and eternal each and every day. It is as simple as saying the words from memory, but also as rich as taking each line—even each word—and letting God speak through them to develop in us the lifestyle and faith of someone who turns their world upside right.

Father, speak to me through Your Word. As I meditate on the Lord's Prayer, give me revelation into each line and phrase so that I may become bolder and more effective in prayer. Let Your kingdom come and transform my life and those in my sphere of influence. Let Your will be done in and through me. In Jesus's name, amen.

June 27

Your Unique Relationship With God

Now it came to pass, as He was praying in a certain place, when He ceased, that one of His disciples said to Him, "Lord, teach us to pray."

—Luke 11:1

The disciples had certainly seen Jesus's persistence in prayer, but the idea that they could go into prayer and then come back with the answer they needed was new. Certainly they were aware the patriarchs had prayed and conversed with God just as Adam and Eve had in the Garden of Eden, but those individuals were special, weren't they? God had called them into those unique relationships with Himself. Could it really be that God wanted the same kind of relationship with each of the disciples? Jesus taught them the answer was yes.

Father, You see me and You know me and You will never forget me. You have engraved my name on the palm of Your hand. Before You formed me in my mother's womb, You knew me. I am Yours, and You are mine. I will not doubt Your love for me. I am Your sheep and You laid down Your life for me; there is no greater love than that. Thank You, Father, for Your extravagant love for me. You protect me, guide me, and crown me with favor. Like the psalmist I will sing of Your love forever. In Jesus's name, amen.

Let God Be Your Father

Have you forgotten how good parents treat children, and that God regards you as his children?
—Hebrews 12:5, The Message

The beginning of confidence in prayer is realizing there is Someone on the other end who not only wants the best for you, but also wants the same relationship with you that a parent has with a child. He wants to see you born whole, admiring your every little finger and toe; to see you grow; to see you learn to walk; to see you learn to fend for yourself; and to never be farther away than a phone call or a text message as you mature and go out to fulfill your purpose in the "family business." He wants to hear what you have to say. He wants to see your needs met. He wants to give you understanding, wisdom, and revelation, and He wants to meet your friends. He always has your back, He always has wise advice for you, He has words of encouragement and edification, and He has the power of the universe to use on your behalf when He sees fit. All you have to do is make the connection with Him.

This is love: not that I love You, but that You loved me so much You sent Jesus to die for me. Father, I receive Your love for me. Deepen my relationship with You and draw me closer to Your heart. In Jesus's name, amen.

June 29

Sanctify Your Desires

Delight yourself also in the Lord, and He shall give you the desires of your heart. Commit your way to the Lord, trust also in Him, and He shall bring it to pass.
—Psalm 37:4–5

Delighting in the Lord is the right path not only to getting the desires of our heart but also of sanctifying the desires themselves. God will not just give us what we want; He will make us desire what He wants—give us His desires—so that following Him is that much more joyful and fulfilling. Some things will fall away as we pray for them because we realize they were never right for us in the first place. To put it simply, the more you hang out with God, the more He rubs off on you—and the more He will rub off on how you do your work, how you relate to your family members and friends, and how you make your decisions. Spend enough time with Him, and suddenly your desires start to look a lot like His.

Father, I delight myself in You. Cause me to desire what You want for me. Bring into divine alignment everything that is misaligned. Superimpose Your will over my plans and preferences. I release You to prune me so that I can be more fruitful for Your kingdom. I must decrease; You must increase. In the name of Jesus, amen.

It's About Two-Way Prayer

My sheep recognize my voice. I know them, and they follow me.
—John 10:27, The Message

Two-way prayer is asking God for or about something and then receiving His answer. It is a conversation. Yet in order for that conversation to take place, our spiritual ears must mature enough for us to discern God's voice from all of the others that speak into our heads and our lives. There is more to prayer than most people think. We must do work within ourselves in order to become mature enough to talk to our Father as a friend and partner.

Thank You for teaching me to know Your voice. Father, open any barrier that would prevent clear communication from Your Spirit to my mind. Lord, clear away anything keeping You from having unrestricted access to my mind, soul, and spirit, and cause our communication to flow freely. In the name of Jesus, amen.

July

July 1

Learn a New Way

Therefore, if anyone is in Christ, he is a new creation. The old has passed away; behold, the new has come.
—2 Corinthians 5:17, ESV

As our spirits start to mature and God draws back from us enough to let us begin growing toward responsible citizenship in His kingdom, we are faced with the same problem as someone who relocates to a new country and culture. We will have to learn a new language, a new way of doing things, and even a new way of thinking, or else we will never succeed in the new country, no matter how well versed we are in the old.

Father, I declare that my spirit is open to the new opportunities and new and pleasant places You are bringing me to in this season. I decree and declare that I will speak the new language You want me to speak and think in the new ways You direct me to think. I will succeed in this new territory. I thank You, Father, for counting me worthy to be relocated to this new place. Thank You for drawing back from me just enough to allow me to grow and mature into the new creation You designed me to be. I decree and declare that I will not return to the old ways, old paths, or old creature I was. I am moving forward in You. In the name of Jesus, amen.

July 2

Embrace the New

For to be carnally minded is death, but to be spiritual minded is life and peace.
—Romans 8:6

The culture we grew up with will always hold us back unless we are willing to let it go to embrace the new. We are stretched, as if by wild horses, between our two worlds. If we try to straddle one foot in the finite, physical world and the other in the infinite, spiritual world, we easily become people of two minds. We can be people of carnal desires with spiritual ambitions. But one realm must have control and dictate our actions in the other. We will never have the discipline in the natural to do the impossible if we do not keep the spiritual in its proper place of precedence.

Father, in the name of Jesus I speak death to my carnal mind. I speak death to any double-mindedness in my spirit that would cause me to straddle between the flesh and the spirit. I release my old mind-set and thought patterns and embrace the new. I choose to be spiritually minded. I choose to dwell in an abundance of life and peace. I declare that I will not be stretched and pulled between two worlds. I live only for You, God. In the name of Jesus, amen.

July 3

Are You Childlike?

Unless you are converted and become as little children, you will by no means enter the kingdom of heaven. Therefore whoever humbles himself as this little child is the greatest in the kingdom of heaven.

—Matthew 18:3–4

Until we can embrace the childlike faith that "with God all things are possible" (Matt. 19:26), we will forever be limited in what we can accomplish. How many people of God today are limited in this way by wisdom that comes from the world and keeps them childish and selfish instead of childlike—humbly and openly embracing the possibilities of God that allow them to grow into the fullness of maturity in Christ?

My Father and my God, I humble myself before You and come to You as a child, believing that with You all things are possible. Father, I declare that I will not be limited by the wisdom that comes from the world in what I can accomplish. You said in Your Word that all things are possible; therefore I have the faith to believe that the impossible is possible in every area of my life. I will not be limited by man. I reject childishness and selfishness, but I receive into my spirit childlike humility. I openly embrace all of Your possibilities and will grow into the fullness of maturity in Christ. In Jesus's name, I speak this into my reality.

July 4

Childish or Childlike?

But the wisdom that is from above is first pure, then peaceable, gentle, willing to yield, full of mercy and good fruits, without partiality and without hypocrisy.
—James 3:17

There is a big difference between being childish and childlike. The first is self-absorbed, lazy, and undisciplined; the second lays down one's own wisdom and position for that which comes from above, leaning not to one's own understanding (Prov. 3:5), and is disciplined by a love that "bears all things, believes all things, hopes all things, endures all things" (1 Cor. 13:7). It's like the story of the emperor's new clothes. To be childlike is to have the simple, frank honesty of a child to realize that sometimes the doctrines we are dressing ourselves up in are nothing more than air and hubris. Instead we must earnestly seek to develop and discipline our senses in the spirit that we might become more proficient in the reality of spiritual things. This cannot be done without a prayer life that is active, unrelenting, and thriving.

Father, I reject any manifestation of a childish spirit that would cause me not to live authentically. I will seek to discipline myself in the ways of the kingdom of God. I decree and declare that through my active, unrelenting prayer life, I will see good fruit established in my life in the name of Jesus. Amen.

July 5

God Still Speaks

For though by this time you ought to be teachers, you need someone to teach you again the first principles of the oracles of God; and you have come to need milk and not solid food.
—Hebrews 5:12–14

If we took a survey, I would bet that far more than half of Christians would either say they believe God doesn't speak to people today as He did during biblical times or that His voice comes only through tradition, the words of Scripture, or the leaders of their churches. I imagine most believers would say He rarely speaks to the common person sitting in a pew. Not only that, but there are also tens of thousands of different ways in which this is taught. Sadly, that equals hundreds of millions of believers who will never grow up into what God has for them—and the world we live in is the worse for it.

I declare that today I hear, receive, understand, and am committed to the oracles of God. God speaks to me, and I listen and follow His commands. I decree and declare that there is a clear and direct channel between heaven and me. I hunger for the meat of God's Word because it brings me life. In the name of Jesus, amen.

Plug Into Heavenly Headquarters

But seek first the kingdom of God and His righteousness, and all these things shall be added to you.
—Matthew 6:33

Too many of us as Christians are ineffective in our missions because of a disconnect between heaven and earth. We are not plugged into the heavenly headquarters that is trying to coordinate our individual part in God's overall strategies and campaigns. Toddlers don't transform kingdoms—at least not in good ways. If we want to plug into the purposes, plans, and victory strategies of heaven, then we have to endure the rigors of the boot camp of prayer and pass its obstacle courses and challenges with flying colors.

Father, today I declare that I will seek Your kingdom first. Your will and Your ways take precedence over mine. I open up the heavens and release Your kingdom and righteousness to reign in my life. You have uniquely designated for my life. By the authority I have in Christ, I declare that I will fulfill every plan, level of success, thought, idea, goal, ambition, and dream that has been planted in me by the hand of the Lord in the name of Jesus. Amen.

July 7

Reach Your Full Potential

My son, do not regard lightly the discipline of the Lord, nor be weary when reproved by him. For the Lord disciplines the one he loves, and chastises every son whom he receives.
—Hebrews 12:5–6, esv

Good parents and good coaches want their children or members of their team to reach their full potential. Success in life and victory on the field of competition depend on competence and excellence. Good parents don't want their kids to grow up physically but continue living in the basement because they don't have self-discipline. These parents will never abandon their children, but they also want them to have lives, loves, and children of their own. God wants the same things for each of His children.

My Father and my God, I thank You for Your discipline and correction that is pushing me to reach my full potential. I open myself to receive the success and victory Your chastisement brings. I speak competence and excellence to my spirit. I call forth discipline into my life that I may be able to sustain high levels of success and accomplishment for the kingdom of God. I decree and declare growth and expansion to be released into my life, in the name of Jesus!

Keep in Contact With God

We should no longer be children, tossed to and fro and carried about by every wind of doctrine...but, speaking the truth in love, may grow up in all things into Him who is the head—Christ.

—Ephesians 4:14–15

If we kids are going to stay in "the family business," we need to keep in close contact with God. We can't just come by on Sundays for brunch; at the minimum, we should be receiving daily instructions, if not hourly. If we are doing something truly world changing, then we should be communicating even more frequently than that. We should have regular planning meetings and strategy summits with God and one another. We should be in constant two-way communication about every detail of what needs to be done along the way. We should endure the times of silence in prayer as well as the times of overflowing revelation. It is only when we can do this that nothing shall be impossible for us.

Father, I declare that my spirit is open to Your instructions today. I speak to the heavens and command them to be open to me with no interference so that I may hear directly from You. I welcome my daily, if not hourly, meetings with You. I receive the overwhelming overflow of revelation I will gain during my times of prayer. I declare that because of this I will accomplish the impossible in Jesus's name. Amen.

July 9

Your Living, Breathing Father

Abba, Father, all things are possible for you. Remove this cup from me. Yet not what I will, but what you will.
—Mark 14:36, ESV

As we submit to the Father's authority and grow under it, He leads by virtue rather than demanding obedience like a dictator threatening punishment. He is no idle idol; He is a living, breathing Father we touch base with every day and have access to every moment. As a loving Daddy, He longs to provide our hearts' desires but will never give us something He knows will hurt us.

My Father and my God, I submit myself to Your authority today and declare that my spirit will grow and become fruitful as You lead me by the virtue of Your flawless character. I submit to Your wisdom as You freely give to me my heart's desires. I align my heart with Your heart and my will with Your will. May Your blessings overtake me and the boundary lines fall for me in pleasant places as You have decreed. In Jesus's name I declare that this is so.

July 10

How Do You Ask?

If you then, being evil, know how to give good gifts to your children, how much more will your heavenly Father give the Holy Spirit to those who ask Him!
—Luke 11:13

Think about going to your father when you want him to give you something. The way you ask matters even more than what you want, doesn't it? Not only does a good father demand the "magic words" of *please* and *thank you,* but also if you ask casually, chances are he won't think you are serious, so he won't give you what you want right away. He will wait to see if you ask again. He wants to see if you are willing to work for it and show yourself responsible enough to handle it. If a child asks disrespectfully or selfishly, how is the father going to respond? If even earthly fathers know that giving children something when they are disrespectful is bad for them, how much more does our heavenly Father know it?

Father, according to Your Word I declare that all Your promises to me are yes and amen. I thank You, God, for giving me good gifts, and for freely giving me the Holy Spirit, who empowers me to pray effectively and strategically according to Your perfect will for my life. God, I thank You, and I praise You for who You are. In Jesus's name, amen.

July 11

You Need to Mature

When I was a child, I spoke as a child, I understood as a child, I thought as a child; but when I became a man, I put away childish things.
—1 Corinthians 13:11

Sometimes God's answer to our prayer is as much in the nature of the asker as in the asking. As Spider-Man's uncle told him, "With great power comes great responsibility." Would a good father ever give great power to someone who shows no responsibility? This is the maturing process that happens in prayer. Sometimes we ask, and in return we are asked to do something rather than receive an immediate answer. Is this a no? Not really. It is more of a "let's give it some time and we will see." There are so many things God wants to give, but until we mature in the faith and in our character enough to show that we can handle these gifts, it would be irresponsible for Him to do so.

I decree and declare in the name of Jesus that I am maturing in the faith and in character. I command my flesh to submit to the obedience of Christ. I command all barricades seeking to stunt my growth to be rendered powerless over my life. I put away the childish things and move to new levels of responsibility, competence, power, and authority. In Jesus's name, amen.

All God's Gifts Are Good

Every good gift and every perfect gift is from above, and comes down from the Father of lights, with whom there is no variation or shadow of turning.
—James 1:17

God doesn't give mixed blessings. There is no dark side to God's gifts. There is no apparent blessing that will ultimately turn into a curse. However, if we stay in close contact with Him and on the course He sets before us, there will be nothing we can't ultimately accomplish.

Father God, I thank You that Your gifts are good. I thank You that Your blessing brings wealth and adds no sorrow to it. Your gifts are free and irreversible. What You have for me is for me and cannot be taken without permission. Therefore I exact my superior authority in Christ and declare to the enemy to take His hands off what is mine. I decree and declare that the blessings of the Lord will overtake me. I decree and declare that my storehouse will overflow and my vats will be filled with new wine in the name of Jesus. Every good and perfect gift that God has portioned to me will be poured out to me. In Jesus's name I pray, amen.

July 13

Living in God's Strength

Not by might nor by power, but by My Spirit.
—Zechariah 4:6

Do you have a dream from God that people have told you is impossible to realize? If you are not getting power from God to live every day in that dream, then you are living in your own strength, not God's. If you're not actively aware of your shortcomings in accomplishing what God has put on your heart and not seeking Him daily for the wisdom and character to see it come into fruition, then what are you doing? Worldly wisdom will never right the world system. Only the wisdom and power of heaven can do that!

Father, Your Word declares that You will speak to me in dreams and visions, and what You have revealed to me for my life will prosper according to Your Word. I come to You for supernatural strength and power to live out that dream every day. Father, I open my spirit to Your Spirit that my shortcomings may be tested, refined, and corrected, so I may complete the mission You have assigned me. The dreams that I have are Your dreams. I declare that nothing will stop the dreams You have placed in my heart. You will see them through to completion. In the name of Jesus, amen.

Live as a Child of God

For as many as are led by the Spirit of God, these are sons of God.
—Romans 8:14

Prayer is the conduit to whatever we need to turn this world upside right, because it is in prayer that we become the children of God—by getting in step with the leadership of the Holy Spirit. How do people know you are a child of God? They see evidence that you are led by His Spirit, which gives way to miraculous things that happen around you. That is why the apostle Paul told us we needed to "pray without ceasing" (1 Thess. 5:17). You can't be led by someone you never hear from or take the time to talk with.

Father, I decree and declare that I am known as a child of God because I bear Your fruit in my life. I take time to talk with You, listen to Your voice, and heed Your instructions. I decree and declare over myself that my spirit is full of the wisdom and discernment of God and that I will steward these blessings with excellence to the glory of Your name. I thank You, God, that Your generous gifts are equipping me to accomplish and achieve the impossible. In the name of Jesus, amen.

July 15

What Are You Working For?

For I, the Lord your God, will hold your right hand, saying to you, "Fear not, for I will help you."
—Isaiah 41:13

If we don't truly have instruction and strength from heaven for what we are doing periodically throughout the day, then who are we really working for? If we don't rely on God's abilities and wisdom every minute of every day to accomplish the tasks before us, whose strength are we operating under? Do we really think we can work without God's incredible power to overcome the problems our world faces? If it is something we can accomplish without needing to pray every thirty minutes or so, if we can in essence do it in our own strength and wisdom, are we really striving to accomplish anything that significant?

Father, in the name of Jesus I decree and declare that I wait patiently to hear instructions from heaven. I put a demand on the resources of heaven. You are the source of my strength. I declare that my spirit is open and ready to receive from You. I decree and declare that my spirit is full of the wisdom and discernment of God and that I will steward these blessings with excellence. Thank You, God, for equipping me to achieve the impossible. In Jesus's name, amen.

You Have Permission to Ask

[There is] one God and Father of all, who is above all, and through all, and in you all.
—Ephesians 4:6

As members of God's family we have the right to go to our Father and ask for His plans, strategies, and resources to fulfill our mission, assignments, and purposes on the earth. Prayer is the conduit that not only reveals the will of God for our individual lives, but it also helps make us the people we need to be to do the impossible on the earth. It's time to plug into that power like we never have before.

Father, You said that because of what Jesus did on the cross I can come boldly before Your throne of grace, that there is no longer any dividing wall to keep me from entering Your presence. I come boldly before You today seeking Your plans, strategies, and resources to fulfill my assignment on the earth. I open my mind and heart to receive downloads from Your Spirit, and I submit to Your discipline so I will become mature and perfectly equipped to do the impossible. I decree and declare that I will not veer off course; I will fulfill my purpose. By Your grace I will walk in Your original plan for my life. In the name of Jesus, amen.

July 17

What's the Purpose of Your Request?

So He said to them, "When you pray, say: Our Father in heaven, hallowed be Your name."
—Luke 11:2

In the second line of the prayer Jesus teaches His disciples, we are given the litmus test of answered prayer: Is the purpose of the request to honor God? Does it magnify His name upon the earth? Are we asking selfishly for our own glory or for the glory of God? When we pray, "Hallowed be Your name," it is an act of worship. However, even more than that, it is saying, "May every request that follows in this prayer be for Your glory and Your glory alone."

Father, in the name of Jesus I open the gates to my heart and give you access to purify my motives. I long to honor You in all I do. If there be any wrong way in me, Father, weed it out. I surrender to Your refining fire so my heart will be pure. Let there be a divine exchange: my will for Yours, my ways for Yours, my words for Yours. I submit my plans and agenda to You. I take command of my flesh and lay down all pride and selfish ambition. I decree and declare that I live for Your glory alone. In the name of Jesus, amen.

Are You Dialed In?

Now this is the confidence that we have in Him, that if we ask anything according to His will, He hears us. And if we know that He hears us, whatever we ask, we know that we have the petitions that we have asked of Him.
—1 John 5:14–15

If there is a problem with our prayers being answered, it is on our end, not on God's. There is nothing wrong with God's broadcast signal, but unless we are tuned in correctly, we are not going to receive it. If you have been wondering why your prayers remain unanswered, here is your answer. You need to persevere until you have correctly dialed into God's frequency of answers. Prayer is answered only when its ultimate motive is the magnification and glorification of God.

Father, I know that You hear and answer prayer. Remove anything that would hinder my ability to hear from You. In the name of Jesus I command the lines of communication to be opened so I can receive from heaven without interference. All the answers I need are found in You, so I will seek You for divine insight. I will press in until I enter into communion with You. Circumcise my heart, Father, so that my heart is right before You and my motive in prayer is only to glorify and magnify You. In the name of Jesus, amen.

July 19

The Power of Worship

Praise God in his sanctuary.... Praise him with trumpet sound; praise him with lute and harp! Praise him with tambourine and dance; praise him with strings and pipe! Praise him with sounding cymbals; praise him with loud clashing cymbals!
—Psalm 150:1–5, ESV

I truly believe breakthroughs are made in the spirit as we lift our voices and our hands to God, showing Him we are not ashamed to shout His name and stand up for Him upon the earth. But worship only begins when the church gathers together to praise His name. If we don't take our worship from the church into the streets and to where we live, our worlds are never going to change. Until we live our worship of God every minute of every day of every week, we are just playacting.

Your Word says that You ordained praise to silence the enemy. Father, in the name of Jesus bring breakthrough in the spirit as I praise and worship You. Release every resource that I need to fulfill my assignment. In the name of Jesus I declare that my praise will not begin on Sunday morning and end when I leave church. I will worship You with my life every minute of every day of the week. I decree and declare that my worship is not a song; it's a lifestyle that touches the world around me. In the name of Jesus, amen.

Grow in Virtue

Make every effort to supplement your faith with virtue, and virtue with knowledge, and knowledge with self-control, and self-control with steadfastness, and steadfastness with godliness, and godliness with brotherly affection, and brotherly affection with love.

—2 Peter 1:5–7, esv

It is not about the medals and glory—for the glory belongs to the Lord God alone—but about bringing the kingdom of God to bear on the kingdoms of this world through prayer. We can never accomplish this if we lack the virtues of a general of prayer: godly wisdom, honesty, kindness, courage, and living lives of disciplined devotion rather than being driven by the latest wind of doctrine or whim of desire.

Father, I desire to partner with You to bring Your kingdom to bear on the kingdoms of the world. Mature me in Your Word and sharpen my sensitivity to Your Spirit. Let wisdom, honesty, kindness, courage, and disciplined devotion mark my life and my prayers. I decree and declare that I will not be motivated by the latest spiritual trends or my own whims. I place my flesh in submission to Your Word and declare what You have said in the name of Jesus. All the glory belongs to You. Amen.

July 21

How's Your Integrity?

Whoever walks in integrity walks securely, but he who makes his way crooked will be found out.
—Proverbs 10:9, esv

Living a life of integrity and honor where we work, where we live, and where we play is the backbone of spreading God's kingdom on the earth. It is worship in action. Every act of integrity during the workweek, every step along the extra mile, every impression of excellence we leave on those around us is worship, whether it be through volunteering, working at our jobs, or putting food on the table for our families. It is being every inch of who God has called us to be. It is always growing and being teachable. It is standing up for what is right in a loving way. It is putting God first in everything and seeking His guidance in every endeavor before we do anything else.

Father, I worship You with my life. I decree and declare that I will live authentically and be the person You called me to be. Place within me a teachable spirit. Empower me to stand boldly for Your truth. I commit to seek Your guidance in everything I do because You are my source of wisdom, strength, and supernatural power. Let me be known as a person of integrity. In this way I will spread Your kingdom everywhere I go. In the name of Jesus, amen.

Are You Slipping?

My voice you shall hear in the morning, O Lord; in the morning I will direct it to You, and I will look up.
—Psalm 5:3

Slipping away from God usually starts when we start to skip our regular prayer times. We get up a little late and have to get to work a little early, so we think, "Oh, well, I'll just spend some time in prayer tonight." Then that night we stay up late helping one of our kids with homework, so we say, "I'll just do it in the morning." It could be any number of really important things you need to do. Jesus was not saying that the cares of this world—caring for your family, paying your rent, going to school or a job, working on your car, or any of a hundred other things—are bad. He was saying that we can't afford to let them get in the way of getting our daily instructions from heaven's headquarters!

Father, You are my priority. I declare that as I seek You first, all the resources I need will be added to me—not only material things but also wisdom, favor, and strength. Let nothing keep me from meeting with You daily. I commit to pursue You faithfully that I may walk in Your wisdom and blessing. In the name of Jesus, amen.

July 23

God Truly Cares—for You

Humble yourselves under the mighty hand of God, that He may exalt you in due time, casting all your care upon Him, for He cares for you.
—1 Peter 5:6–7

God doesn't want you to neglect your cares. He wants to help you take care of them. He wants to give you wisdom about how to handle them—whether it is a relationship, a project at work, volunteering at your kids' school, or your passion to see a world issue resolved justly. He wants to give you strength to handle it. He has the wisdom you need to make it right. He wants to see you succeed so that He can be glorified in you.

Father, Your Word says You watch the sparrows and make sure each has its needs met. How much more do you care for me. In the name of Jesus I declare over myself that I will not doubt Your love for me, but I will run to You with every need. You are my source of wisdom. You are the one who renews my strength. It is Your desire that I prosper and be in good health even as my soul prospers. I declare that I will run to You because You are more than able to accomplish everything that concerns me today. In the name of Jesus, amen.

Prayer at the Center

I exhort first of all that supplications, prayers, intercessions, and giving of thanks be made for all men, for kings and all who are in authority, that we may lead a quiet and peaceable life in all godliness and reverence.
—1 Timothy 2:1–2

Prayer is not separated from what we do in the world; rather, it should be at the center of our lives whether we make a salary or pay salaries. If you are called to work in a secular job or run your own business, then you should be relying on God, through prayer and faith, to infuse you with His wisdom and power so that you will reflect Him in your workplace or marketplace.

Father, I decree and declare that I fully rely on You to give me wisdom and power today. On my job, at home, wherever I go, Father, I trust You to lead me in the way I should go. I commit to spend time in prayer and stand in faith on Your promises. Download divine insight so I will know how to conduct the affairs of my day. Breathe into my spirit fresh revelation so I can be on the cutting edge and defy the status quo. Mold me into Your image so my life reflects Your character. Father, let the light of Your love and truth shine through me everywhere I go. In the name of Jesus, amen.

July 25

Remained Tuned In

Pray without ceasing.
—1 Thessalonians 5:17

Prayer is not so much the practice of folding your hands, closing your eyes, and kneeling at the foot of your bed or in a pew as it is an attitude of constantly listening for God's instructions as you go through the day. Brother Lawrence called this "practicing the presence of God." As he put it, "There is not in the world a kind of life more sweet and delightful than that of a continual conversation with God: those only can comprehend it who practice and experience it."[1] What is the key to maintaining this "continual conversation"? Maintaining the attitude of worship in every step of your day. This is what it means to "walk in the Spirit" (Gal. 5:25).

Father, I decree and declare that I will walk in the Spirit and as a result I will not fulfill the lusts of the flesh. Teach me how to "practice Your presence" all day long and remain in an attitude of worship. There is nothing more delightful than being with You. In the name of Jesus I speak to my heart and declare that I desire nothing more than You. I want You more than anything else. Thank You, Father, for promising that as I chase after You, I will be found by You. In the name of Jesus, amen.

July 26

How Do You Respond to Obstacles?

I do not run aimlessly; I do not box as one beating the air. But I discipline my body and keep it under control, lest after preaching to others I myself should be disqualified.
—1 Corinthians 9:26–27, esv

How excellently we live to reflect God's glory back to Him every day is our boot camp of faith, our training ground for the assignment He has for us. When someone is in boot camp, he learns to shine his shoes, keep his bunk immaculate, and show respect to every other soldier around him. It is also where he is tested. In boot camp recruits are presented with obstacles and told to overcome them. If they do, they are presented with bigger obstacles; if they don't, they are sent back to the end of the line to start over again. As God recruits us and begins to work within us for our growth, we face a similar series of obstacle courses to overcome in prayer. How we respond to these situations will show us how large an assignment God can trust us with.

Father, I submit to Your divine boot camp because this is how I will become prepared for the mission I have been given. Empower me, Lord, to overcome each test. I don't want to repeat any obstacles. Cause me to grow in You so I will be fit for my assignment. In the name of Jesus, amen.

July 27

What Does Your Conscience Say?

The goal of our instruction is love from a pure heart and a good conscience and a sincere faith.
—1 Timothy 1:5, NAS

Loving from a good conscience means always obeying your conscience, which is the voice of your human spirit that will either speak from the law written on your heart or from what the Holy Spirit tells it to say. Honest or sincere faith is faith that is not tainted by selfish desires or ungodly ambitions. The basis for all of this is a life where honesty is uncompromisingly pursued, both where others can see it and when no one else is looking but God.

Father, even when no one is looking, let my life reflect Your character. In the name of Jesus increase my knowledge of Your Word and sensitivity to the still, small voice You placed within me. I decree and declare that I will honor You with my words and deeds; my faith is not tainted by selfish or ungodly ambitions. Purify my heart, Lord, so my love for You is not compromised in any way. In Jesus's name, amen.

Walk in Worship

Rejoice always, pray without ceasing, in everything give thanks; for this is the will of God in Christ Jesus for you.
—1 Thessalonians 5:16–18

Being in a continual attitude of rejoicing is the entrance into prayer. Being grateful and filled with thanksgiving is how we come out of it. Then the cycle repeats itself—immediately. The beginning of effective prayer is learning to continually walk in worship, with our main goal always being to increase and experience the glory of God. Without it, we can do nothing; with it, nothing is beyond our doing.

Father, I will bless You at all times; Your praise shall continually be in my mouth. Teach me to remain steadfast in You, continually walking in worship. Father, increase my sensitivity to the supernatural realm. Open my eyes to spiritual realities and allow me to experience Your glory. Without You, I can do nothing, but with You, nothing is impossible. Father, anoint me with Your strength and power as I spend time in Your presence. In the name of Jesus, amen.

July 29

Make His Voice Familiar

For the word of God is living and powerful, and sharper than any two-edged sword, piercing even to the division of soul and spirit, and of joints and marrow, and is a discerner of the thoughts and intents of the heart.
—Hebrews 4:12

Just as you might read several books by the same author in school to become familiar with his "voice," so the Bible is a great place to start learning the way God speaks to us. And I don't mean that you should get comfortable with King James English—I mean to get so familiar with God's character through His Word that, as we might with a close friend or spouse, we know instantly whether or not something we hear is something He would say.

Father, Your Word says Your sheep know Your voice. I decree and declare that as one of Your sheep I am able to discern Your voice. Sharpen my spiritual discernment so that I can hear You more clearly. Unblock the lines of communication between us. I resist and repel all doubt and unbelief now in the name of Jesus. I reject every ungodly opinion that would prevent me from believing what You say. I love Your words and will hide them in my heart that I might not sin against You. In Jesus's name, amen.

July 30

What Is the Source?

If anyone is a hearer of the word and not a doer, he is like a man who looks intently as his natural face in the mirror. For he looks at himself and goes away and at once forgets what he was like. But the one who looks into the perfect law, the law of liberty, and perseveres, being no hearer who forgets but a doer who acts, he will be blessed in his doing.

—James 1:23–25, esv

When a thought comes to mind, where is it coming from—God, evil, your physical urges, or your own psyche? The answer to discerning the difference between these "voices in our heads" is learned through practice and repetition, with the Bible as your personal trainer. It is the mirror into which we look and learn who we truly are. Familiarity with the Word of God is more than memorizing scriptures. The more time we spend reading the Bible, the more it permeates our beings and clarifies the voices within us.

Father, I commit to study Your Word that I might know Your will and Your ways and receive Your divine wisdom. Your laws are good, and Your precepts are right. I declare that I desire them more than gold. I decree and declare that I will not be merely a hearer of the Word; I will act and be blessed in my doing. In the name of Jesus, amen.

July 31

Give It Time

In the morning sow your seed, and at evening withhold not your hand, for you do not know which will prosper, this or that, or whether both alike will be good.
—Ecclesiastes 11:6, esv

There are often months, if not years, of things being cultivated in prayer before they happen "overnight" in the natural. A farmer may reap the harvest in a week, but he first had to devote months to planting, weeding, and cultivating or the crop would never have been as large or as healthy. Planting and cultivating, tilling the soil and preparing it for the next season are all hard work. So oftentimes is prayer.

Father, I decree and declare that I remain fervent in prayer. I do not stop believing when there seems to be no change. I keep tending to the seeds I have sown in prayer and expect a harvest in Your perfect time. I expect the seeds You have planted in me to grow as well. In the name of Jesus I decree and declare that nothing will stop me from reaching the destiny You have planned for me. Even if it takes time, I know Your purposes will prevail. In the name of Jesus, amen.

August

August 1

Build on Your Center

[Christ] is the image of the invisible God, the first-born of all creation.... And he is before all things, and in him all things hold together.
—Colossians 1:15–17, esv

We have become obsessed with our ends—the goals and dreams God gives us in our hearts—but forget about our center—our foundation in Christ that is the strength and source of wisdom that makes those goals and dreams possible. If we do not cling to the center and do everything assigned to us from the center, what does it really matter? If we are doing it in our own strength rather than through His, from the center, is what we are doing really from Him? Or is it just to look better to others or ease our consciences? Are we choosing to pursue our purpose more than we pursue God Himself?

Father, continually remind me today that it is all about You. You are the center of my life. Help me to escape the trap of focusing on my circumstances, my plans, my strengths, and even my weaknesses. Let my focus turn to You as the strength and source of everything in my life. You deserve all glory and honor, and You alone are able to complete that which You started in me. As I keep my eyes on You, lead me into the purpose You have destined for me today. In the name of Jesus, amen.

August 2

Let God Birth It

Continue earnestly in prayer, being vigilant in it with thanksgiving.
—Colossians 4:2

I believe God instructs us to come to Him with our petitions so that He can infuse us with the answers. He needs us to focus on the need or desire so He can put into us the blessings and gifts that will draw the answer into existence. When we go to Him in prayer, He wants us to leave rejoicing, knowing our petitions have been heard and allocated for and that we have changed through the process of receiving His response. We can be assured that help is on the way because the answer has already manifested inside of us. It is just a matter of God allowing it to be birthed into the natural.

Father, You have already provided the answers to my needs. As I wait for the manifestation to be evident around me, I will not walk in fear, anxiety, or stress. I cast all my cares upon You. You are my protection, my provider, my healer, and my hope for the future. Show me if there is anything in my heart that is hindering the fulfillment of what You desire to birth into my life. Create a new heart within me and renew my spirit today that I may walk in the destiny You have prepared for me. In Jesus's name, amen.

August 3

Grab Your Lifeline

And this is the confidence we have toward him, that if we ask anything according to his will he hears us.
—1 John 5:14, esv

One of the ways I think of prayer is the act of calling out to heaven for a lifeline. As we hold firmly to one end of it, keeping it taut, God can use it to slide down the answers to our petitions. When He throws out that line, we grab it in prayer, but if we let go of it before the answer is manifested, we become disconnected from the source of our salvation. Because of this, it is also important to let what you pray govern what comes out of your mouth. Have you ever prayed something in faith only to hear yourself later talking about how impossible the thing is that you are believing for? That is a sign that the answer has not been downloaded into your spirit and that it's time to get back to prayer on that issue.

Father, I resolve today that I will not stop praying until You answer. I will not speak words of doubt or disbelief. When the enemy tries to discourage me, I will remind him that through You everything I need is available to me. I will stand strong in the knowledge that all of my needs are supplied according to Your riches in glory. In Jesus's name, amen.

Prayer Is the Key

Compared to the high privilege of knowing Christ Jesus as my Master, firsthand, everything I once thought I had going for me is insignificant.... I've dumped it all in the trash so that I could embrace Christ and be embraced by him.

—Philippians 3:7–8, The Message

Prayer is the most powerful place of spiritual growth. Sitting in church under good teaching is a wonderful thing, and applying the principles learned there is life transforming, but your pastor can't get to know God for you. You have to take Jesus up on His invitation to come hang out. You have to spend time with your physical eyes closed and your spiritual eyes open, letting Jesus show you what He really wants for you and the plans He has for you to impact your world. It is in this place of intimacy that He hands us the keys to His kingdom.

Father, open my eyes to truly see You today. As I do, make my vision clear and transform me from the inside out. Show me how to be holy as You are holy. As I seek You in prayer, show me the things that break Your heart. Remind me of what really matters to You so that I will accomplish all of the plans You have for me and become all I was born to be. In the name of Jesus, amen.

August 5

Be Like Jesus

And he who searches hearts knows what is the mind of the Spirit, because the Spirit intercedes for the saints according to the will of God.
—Romans 8:27, esv

Do you want to be like Jesus? Then let me ask you a question: What is Jesus doing right now? He's at the right hand of the Father praying—interceding for us and our world. You want to be like Jesus? Then you need to be in prayer. What is the best thing to pray? Find out what Jesus is praying at the right hand of the Father and pray in agreement with Him. Find out what Jesus thinks about matters, and let Him put the words into your mouth to pray. Is there any better person to agree with in prayer than Jesus Himself?

Father, I align myself with Jesus, my great intercessor. I bring every circumstance and relationship in my life into alignment with the words of Jesus. I am not conformed to this world, but I am transformed because His thoughts are renewing my mind. Speak to me and through me today. Let Your light shine through me into a dark world and draw those who are seeking You. I declare that my life shines with Your glory and that I am in agreement with what is being spoken over me in the heavens. In Jesus's name, amen.

August 6

Be the Answer to Your Prayer

I therefore, a prisoner of the Lord, urge you to walk in a manner worthy of the calling to which you have been called, with all humility and gentleness, with patience, bearing with one another in love, eager to maintain the unity of the Spirit in the bond of peace.

—Ephesians 4:1–3, esv

After you have prayed and heard in the big conversation what God's will is, then go out and be part of the manifestation of the word He has given you. Live as an answer to prayer. Live as a citizen and ambassador of the heavenly kingdom.

Father, I decree and declare today that You are releasing divine anointing in my life and that my ability to be the answer to prayer will convince others that Jehovah is the true and living God. You protect me with angelic escorts. You cover my head with the oil of Your Holy Spirit. You fill my ears with good news. You fill my mouth with praise and words of encouragement. You clothe my hands with productivity and free my feet from obstructions. I am able to be an answer to prayer because I am Your workmanship, created in Christ Jesus for good works. I will accomplish everything that You have planned for me today. In Jesus's name, amen.

August 7

How Are You Answering Jesus's Prayer?

I do not pray that You should take them out of the world, but that You should keep them from the evil one. They are not of the world, just as I am not of the world.
—John 17:15–16

When Jesus prayed for His disciples, He wasn't just praying. He also was passing the baton to them and those who would believe in Him in the generations to come. It is one thing for Jesus to pray but quite another for us to come into agreement with that prayer and take up His desires for our generation as if they are our own. Will we be part of the answer to Jesus's prayer or part of the problem by preventing His petitions from coming into reality?

Father, I accept the assignment that Jesus gave when He prayed for all who would follow Him. I declare that the anointing that is on my life will flow unhindered, and it will repel every evil scheme of the enemy. I speak success, prosperity, health, wealth, vision, direction, creativity, holiness, righteousness, peace, and joy from Your Spirit today. I declare that I have everything I need to be part of the answer and not the problem. I am anointed in this season to bring forth kingdom strategies and fulfill divinely ordained assignments. In the name of Jesus, amen.

Prayer as Spiritual Warfare

I exhort first of all that supplications, prayers, intercessions, and giving of thanks be made for all men.... For this is good and acceptable in the sight of God our Savior, who desires all men to be saved and to come to the knowledge of the truth.
—1 Timothy 2:1–4

In many ways praying for others is the cornerstone of spiritual warfare. While God loves humanity, He does not miss the individual trees for the forest. He loves humanity because He loves each and every individual who comprises the vast seas of people who live on the earth. God has a plan for each one of their lives, but He also needs those who know Him to stand in the gap for those who don't and be an advocate to heaven on their behalf.

Father, place the anointing of the prayer warrior upon me. Interrupt my agenda today with those who need Your touch. Give me words for those in need. Give me ears to hear their cries and a heart that is soft enough to feel their pain. I decree complete restoration of anything the enemy has stolen from their lives. By the power of Your Spirit, break every chain of bondage, heal every hurt, meet every need, and restore the hope and joy that come from salvation through Your Son. In Jesus's name, amen.

August 9

SUFFER ON BEHALF OF OTHERS

For I could wish that I myself were accursed from Christ for my brethren, my countrymen according to the flesh.
—ROMANS 9:3

Herein is the agony of battling in prayer as if suffering with others through the dark valley to God's full salvation on the other side. We call upon heaven for them as if we ourselves were going through whatever they are experiencing. This may call for more concentrated times of prayer or even fasting as we seek to hear clearly from heaven on their behalves. We allow the Holy Spirit to make "intercession for us with groanings which cannot be uttered" (Rom. 8:26).

Father, download into my spirit a fresh zeal and excitement for intercession today. I lift up others before you as if their needs were my own. I seek Your thoughts and intentions toward them and declare that You have provided all the answers they need. You have forgiven and cleansed their sins. You have healed their diseases and restored their relationships with their children and families. You have provided them with an abundance of blessing so they might give generously to those in need. You have assigned them a specific destiny and equipped them with every good thing that they might accomplish it. In Jesus's mighty name, amen.

August 10

Find the Peace

Be anxious for nothing, but in everything by prayer and supplication, with thanksgiving, let your requests be made known to God; and the peace of God, which surpasses all understanding, will guard your hearts and minds in Christ Jesus.
—Philippians 4:6–7

As the work of prayer finds its completion, we experience the answer: the grace and authority needed to overcome the difficulty flood like morning light into our spirits and souls. The answer comes in our hearts, and we know without a doubt that the problem is taken care of, even if that answer has not yet manifested in the natural world. It is a hard thing to describe until you have experienced it, but it feels as though the burden of the matter lifts and the peace of God floods your heart and mind.

Father, I declare that Your peace is guarding my heart and mind today. I have a quiet mind that is free from worry and anxiety. I am set free from concerns about my past, present, and future. I decree that a new day is dawning for my life, my family, my job, and my ministry. I am not moved to fear by the circumstances around me because You have hidden me in the shadow of Your wing. I speak, "Peace, be still," and Your Spirit calms the atmosphere around me. Your unshakable peace is my inheritance today. In Jesus's name, amen.

August 11

Train Your Spiritual Sense

But solid food belongs to those who are of full age, that is, those who by reason of use have their senses exercised to discern both good and evil.
—Hebrews 5:14

Spending time reading the Bible, meditating on the scriptures, and praying saturates our conscience with the reality of the spiritual world. It attunes our spiritual senses to hear God's voice, and it hones our instincts to the differences between right and wrong in every matter. As we practice this and our spirits grow toward maturity, our senses are trained to discern between good and evil.

Father, I receive the clarity and insight that Your Spirit gives me concerning both the spiritual world and the physical world. You promise to give me discernment, wisdom, and understanding so that I might rightly divide Scripture and know the difference between truth and lies. Increase my understanding as I seek You today. Reveal anything in my heart that is clouding my judgment or keeping me from fully submitting to Your will and strategy for my life. Give me the strength to let go of anything and everything that keeps me from living life completely in tune with Your voice. I declare now that I will walk in step with Your Spirit today as He leads and guides me into all truth. In Jesus's name, amen.

How Is the Holy Spirit Leading You?

The Helper, the Holy Spirit, whom the Father will send in My name, He will teach you all things, and bring to your remembrance all things that I said to you.

—John 14:26

The Holy Spirit's leading is not a loud, overwhelming voice within us but often an uneasiness or discomfort with following one path—a "check" in our spirit—and a peace or feeling of confidence about moving in another. This is the subtle directing of the Holy Spirit within our human spirits, and the more sensitive and open we are to this inner prompting, the more we will see things in our lives line up as God wants them to.

Father, today I will walk in a new level of intimacy with Your Spirit. Let the anointing that is on my life for this season flow uncontaminated upon my life, filling me with renewed purpose. May it attract only those you have divinely ordained to be a part of the work You are accomplishing through me. I ask You to place the anointing of Samuel upon me that I might walk in new sensitivity and obedience to Your voice. Help me to decrease so that You might increase. May my humility be reflected in my ability to hear Your voice. As I walk in humble obedience to You, let Your Spirit work through me to touch those I come in contact with me today. In Jesus's name, amen.

August 13

You're Not in the Dark

No longer do I call you servants, for a servant does not know what his master is doing; but I have called you friends, for all things that I heard from My Father I have made known to you.
—John 15:15

God doesn't want us to be in the dark about things. Many look at Jesus's praying "not My will, but Yours, be done" (Luke 22:42) in the Garden of Gethsemane and forget that in the one instance He prayed this prayer, it was not because He didn't know the will of God. It was because He was agreeing to do the will of God despite the pain it would cause Him. It was a prayer of consecrating Himself to the tough road ahead to the cross, not Him saying, "Lord, I don't really know what You want in this matter, so please do whatever You think is best."

Father, I agree to do Your will even if it's uncomfortable. I consecrate myself to You. Your Word says Your plans are to give me hope and a future, so I greet today in anticipation of the good things You have prepared for me. Let Your wisdom, understanding, and prophetic insight be upon me today. Cause me to walk in perfect sync with Your will for my life. In the name of Jesus I pray, amen.

God's Will Can Be Known

Therefore do not be foolish, but understand what the will of the Lord is.
—Ephesians 5:17, esv

It takes consistent work and a good deal of growing up spiritually, but God's will is not unfathomable. The mysteries of God are there for us to solve, not for us to throw up our hands at and say, "Well, you never really know, so why worry about it?" They are there to make the pursuit of knowing God that much more exciting. And if being friends with God is not impossible, then what is?

Father, open my ears to the movements of Your Spirit with clear, crisp transmission. I seek an unprecedented level of closeness to Your heart today. Give me assurance that I am in the center of Your will, and do not let my feet falter on the path You have ordained for me. Let not my ears or eyes be seduced by the spirit of covetousness or my mind by the pride of life. Lead me along the path of righteousness for Your name's sake. Show me Your perfect will for my life and give me new ways of living and better strategies. Upgrade my thinking with kingdom methodology, and give me supernatural discipline to implement Your will in my life today. In Jesus's name, amen.

August 15

Endure the Labor Pains

Pray in the Spirit at all times and on every occasion. Stay alert and be persistent in your prayers for all believers everywhere.
—Ephesians 6:18, nlt

The desire to know God and build His kingdom is what causes people to pray hours and hours a day and never get bored. There are things to be birthed in the spirit that will come only after enduring labor pains in prayer. When we pray, there is work to be done in the spirit that will not be done if we stop. Jesus is the cornerstone of the kingdom of God, His Word is the foundation, and prayer is where we receive its blueprints.

Father, I declare new cycles of victory, success, and prosperity will replace old cycles of failure, poverty, and death in my life. As I endure the labor pains of what You are birthing in my life, I stand on the promise that everything that pertains to my life and godliness must be released in its correct time and season. I command everything to be released in Jesus's name. Since Your Word is a lamp unto my feet and a light unto my path, I will not stumble or fall. I declare my relationships are restored, my health is renewed, and my finances are rejuvenated as I step out in faith and actively bring Your promises to life today. In Jesus's name, amen.

What's Your Prayer Lifestyle?

Continue steadfastly in prayer, being watchful in it with thanksgiving.
—Colossians 4:2, ESV

I don't want to put a guilt trip on you about how much time you spend in prayer. The fact that some people pray in concentrated, focused seclusion for hours a day doesn't mean God will lead every Christian to do that. The Bible doesn't give specific guidelines for how long and how often we should pray for a reason—and that is because we are to be led by the Spirit of God in prayer as in everything else in life. There may be times when you pray for hours in a day and other times when you simply say short prayers throughout the day. On some days prayer will feel like mining though rock, and other days it will be "joy inexpressible and full of glory" (1 Pet. 1:8). The point is we need to be dedicated to prayer.

Father, I declare progress in my prayer life. The bondage of guilt over past mistakes will not keep me from learning more of You in prayer today. As I commune with You, reveal more of Yourself to me today and cause divine winds of the Holy Spirit to blow. Dismantle any evil powers working to frustrate my day, and take Your rightful place as the top priority in my life. In the name of Jesus, amen.

August 17

Be Practiced and Prepared

He who is faithful in what is least is faithful also in much; and he who is unjust in what is least is unjust also in much.

—Luke 16:10

We need to learn to operate in prayer through the small, everyday realities of life so that when God calls us to address the big, once-in-a-lifetime events, we are already practiced and prepared. We won't learn to pray down miracles until we've learned to pray down our daily bread. And we won't be disciplined in the things of the Spirit until we have learned to be disciplined in the natural.

Father, I decree that I will be found faithful with all that You have given me so that You might raise me up in due season and enlarge my territory. May I be found trustworthy in Your sight. May the anointing You have placed upon my life repel any schemes of the wicked. Synchronize my actions today with Your perfect will and agenda. Purify my motives, and let me be a shining example of Your love, mercy, and grace to my generation. Give me divine discipline so that everything my hand touches will prosper for Your glory. In Jesus's name, amen.

August 18

How's Your Calendar?

If you have not been faithful in the unrighteous mammon [or worldly wealth], who will commit to your trust the true riches?
—Luke 16:11

If you want to check a person's level of commitment and spirituality, there are four areas you should examine: how they manage their daily calendar, their finances, their relationships, and their destiny. These four areas make up the difference between a truly rich life and a life that is in spiritual poverty. Do you live each day maximizing your assets or making excuses for living beyond your means? Are you giving into the lives of others, or are you always the one in need of being comforted, advised, or helped out of a jam? Are you still waiting for that big break before you really get down to living the life you want to live, or are you enjoying each day for the challenges and successes it presents, seeing it as an opportunity to enjoy, grow, and build toward a better future?

Father, I declare that my decisions today will change the trajectory of my future and bring it into alignment with Your plans for me. Wherever I place my feet, I walk in Your authority and expand my territory for Your name's sake. Increase my productivity and efficiency and give me the anointing of Solomon to wisely manage my resources today. In Jesus's name, amen.

August 19

What Can You Do With What You Have?

Prepare your outside work, make it fit for yourself in the field; and afterward build your house.
—Proverbs 24:27

I hope you realize that what you do with what you have today will do more for your destiny than waiting for someday when you have won the lottery or hit it big in some way. The truth of the matter is that waiting for a "someday when" never takes you anywhere. Everything you need to accomplish the dreams and goals in your heart is already in your hands, and only by investing it today will you have what you need to accomplish tomorrow's hopes and aspirations.

Father, I seek divine opportunities to advance Your kingdom today. I move boldly toward my destiny and refuse to be distracted by insignificant things. The blessings of the Lord will follow me today, and I am loaded with benefits. I am living my most blessed and best day today. I declare that I am purpose driven, kingdom principled, success oriented, and I work according to Your agenda. You are my partner and give me everything I need to assist me in the fulfillment of my kingdom assignment during this season. In Jesus's name, amen.

Preparation Meets Opportunity

Then he [Elisha] said, "Take the arrows"; so he [Joash, the king of Israel] took them. And he said to the king of Israel, "Strike the ground"; so he struck three times, and stopped. And the man of God was angry with him, and said, "You should have struck five or six times; then you would have struck Syria till you had destroyed it! But now you will strike Syria only three times."

—2 Kings 13:18–19

The greatest value of our lives comes from what we do with our time, and the only time we really have control over is the current moment. There are no "overnight" successes, only people whose preparation met God-given opportunity. While the opportunities and favor in our lives come from the Lord, the preparation is up to us.

Father, You are equipping me with not only supernatural gifts and abilities but also character. My life will bring You glory because I have waited for your preparation to be complete. I confess today that the fruit of the Spirit characterize my life. You have divine appointments and opportunities lined up for me today, and I am working in perfect harmony with Your plan. I will be in the right place at the right time with all of the right relationships and resources I need because You have called me and anointed me with purpose. In the name of Jesus, amen.

August 21

Are You Ready?

Go to the ant, you sluggard! Consider her ways and be wise, which, having no captain, overseer or ruler, provides her supplies in summer, and gathers her food in the harvest.
—Proverbs 6:6–8

There will be amazing opportunities in our lives, but will you be ready for them? Have you spent the thousands of hours when no one else was looking making the proper preparations? Are you using your time today to invest in something worthwhile or doing barely enough to get by?

Father, I declare that I am ready to step into my destiny today. I will not listen to those who try to kill my dreams or fill my mind with doubts and intimidation. I arise today through the mighty strength of Your sovereignty, grace, divinity, and knowledge that I was born within this generation to contribute something significant. I am not here by accident. You have placed me here to fulfill Your purpose. Let Your Spirit be with me, before me, behind me, in me, beneath me, above me, on my right, on my left, when I sit down, when I arise, when I speak, in my business dealings, negotiations, communications, crossing borders, and when I retire for the night. In Jesus's name, amen.

August 22

How Are You Giving Your All?

Do you see a man who excels in his work? He will stand before kings; he will not stand before unknown men.
—Proverbs 22:29

Every day, whether we are a student, a burger flipper in a fast-food restaurant, or the president of a Fortune 500 company, we have opportunities to excel at what we are doing—to make an investment to get better at something. We can work and give our all to improve ourselves, or we can sit back and loaf.

Father, I declare that all of my God-given goals are achievable. As I step out in faith, completely surrendered to Your will, increase my fruitfulness and bless me with victory over my circumstances. You have given me courage to walk out my convictions today and impact every sphere of my influence. You have created me to make a difference in this world, and I hold nothing back from my service to Your kingdom. Let holiness and righteousness be my reputation, and use my testimony—even the parts of my past that caused pain and suffering—for your glory. Let my good works today memorialize the wondrous love and mercy of God and let my life be characterized by excellence, integrity, credibility, and honesty. In Jesus's name, amen.

August 23

Enjoy Your Daily Bread

Give us this day our daily bread.
—Matthew 6:11

Are you waiting for your ship to come in? Well, guess what. It already has! All you will ever need for your prosperity—and pouring out a blessing on the earth—is already at your fingertips. Your "daily bread" is already in your hands. What are you going to do with it?

Father, today You have blessed me beyond measure. All that I have is Yours, and I am eternally grateful for every good and perfect gift that comes from above. My blessings, like the stars, are too numerous to count. Health and wealth walk with me, hand in hand. My victories are as abundant as the grains of sand. Lack and struggle are distant memories of the past. My enemies are subdued. I am fruitful in all my endeavors, and Your provision fills my life in every way to overflowing. Your blessings come upon me and overtake me. I have more than enough. I thank You. In Jesus's name, amen.

Living in Surety

[Be] rejoicing in hope, patient in tribulation, continuing steadfastly in prayer.
—Romans 12:12

Do we persevere in prayer ourselves? Do we value our relationship with God more than life itself? Or are we sidetracked by doubts and distractions? There is a certain degree of trial and error in coming to know God with this kind of surety. Too many give up on it or accept the teaching that knowing God in this way is only meant for a chosen few. Another problem is that in order to be close to God, we must walk a path that takes us out of ourselves and demands that we leave behind the baggage of hang-ups, doubt, self-centeredness, destructive habits, addictions, and hatred. Though the path is well marked, it is a journey we must master on our own.

Father, nothing can separate me from Your love. I can boldly let go of my past and face whatever challenges lie ahead because You have filled my soul with joy and peace and my heart with courage. Wherever I go today, I bring Your healing and comfort into the atmosphere. Shield me from persecution and false accusation, from temptation and compromise. I arise today knowing my salvation is sure because of the finished work of Christ at Calvary. In Jesus's name, amen.

August 25

You Needn't Work Alone

Be of the same mind toward one another. Do not set your mind on high things, but associate with the humble. Do not be wise your own opinion.
—Romans 12:16

The bigger the vision God gives you, the more likely it is that God has called others to work beside you in fulfilling it. It is likely, in fact, that you will not even be the leader in the endeavor. God commonly tests our dedication to His plan by seeing if we will be faithful in helping someone else accomplish the vision He has given him or her.

Father, show me the cause You are assigning me to champion today. I will responsibly utilize the gifts You have given me to be a blessing to my family, community, and nation. You have divinely placed me in a position to help others accomplish their God-given dreams. I am able to give my time, talent, and financial resources to charitable and nonprofit organizations whose focus is on helping the less fortunate, the orphan, widow, indigent, homeless, destitute, and helpless. I have more than enough and can give to those who can never repay the favor. Increase my networking abilities and help me to rally support for the accomplishment of other people's God-given visions and dreams. In the name of Jesus, amen.

August 26

The Power of Two

If two of you agree on earth concerning anything that they ask, it will be done for them by My Father in heaven.
—Matthew 18:19

Imagine for a moment the unlimited power of a husband and wife who walk constantly in agreement—the power of a mother and father united in the raising of children who understand the power of relationships, are saturated in wisdom, and are full of faith! How different would our world be today if there were more couples like this? How different would the church be? How different would our communities be? How different would our nations be?

Father, Your Word says one person can put a thousand to flight and two can chase off ten thousand. Strengthen the hedge of protection around my marriage and family and whisper peace into my relationships, ministry, workplace, and business. No evil shall come near to my dwelling place or my marriage. Cause my relationships to work in perfect harmony with You today. Break any unhealthy patterns in our relationship, guard our thoughts and words, and fill us with new levels of passion and zeal for your calling upon us as a couple. Remove every hindrance from the divinely ordained intimacy and unity You intend for our relationship. In Jesus's name, amen.

August 27

Walk in Love

Love suffers long and is kind; love does not envy; love does not parade itself, is not puffed up; does not behave rudely, does not seek its own, is not provoked, thinks no evil; does not rejoice in iniquity, but rejoices in the truth; bears all things, believes all things, hopes all things, endures all things. Love never fails.

—1 Corinthians 13:4–8

Take a moment to look at the passage above again, but this time, in every place where it says "love," replace that word with your name. That's you walking in love. That's you walking in proactive forgiveness. That's you cherishing your relationships over your things; over your accomplishments, goals, and tasks; and over yourself. That's you living the richest life possible.

Father, I declare today that Your love gives me the patience to suffer long and yet be kind. Your love causes me not to envy, parade myself, or be puffed up. Because of Your love, I will not behave rudely or seek to fulfill my own selfish desires. Your love keeps me from thinking angry and malicious thoughts about others. I do not rejoice in sinfulness but rejoice in the truth. With Your love I bear all things, believe all things, hope all things, and endure all things. I am secure that Your love never fails. In the name of Jesus, amen.

What You Do With Today Matters

Have you commanded the morning since your days began, and caused the dawn to know its place?
—Job 38:12

Today has a place in eternity that no other day can take. There are things God has established for you to accomplish this day, and there are things the devil has set up to distract you. Certainly there is some leeway in this, and God gives an incredible amount of grace, but what we do with today matters, not only for ourselves but also for those God has appointed for us to touch.

Father, I do not take today for granted. Download fresh vision and purpose into my spirit today so that I might take advantage of every opportunity You bring my way. I have a fresh anointing for the day ahead that is uncontaminated and uncompromised. By this anointing, every yoke is broken off of my life and every burden is lifted. Your yoke is easy, and Your burden is light. I declare that a new cycle of power and victory in my life begins right now. I break free from the cares of yesterday and will not take on any worries about tomorrow, for You have given me grace that is sufficient for each day in and of itself. Your mercies are new every morning, and You clothe me with newness of purpose as I wait upon You. In Jesus's name, amen.

August 29

What Is Sin, Really?

Let us lay aside every weight, and the sin which so easily ensnares us, and let us run with endurance the race that is set before us, looking unto Jesus, the author and finisher of our faith.
—Hebrews 12:1–2

Sin is not just about great moral failure; it is more about the general failure of fulfilling our mission and assignment from God. Look at what the writer of Hebrews says about temptation and the race God has called us to run. He sets Jesus as our example. Jesus was without sin because He knew that even one small sin would have defeated Him in the race His Father set before Him. And because Jesus lived without sin, we have access to the forgiveness of our sins and therefore have the ability to run the race God has set before us unencumbered by their entanglements.

Father, today I confess and receive forgiveness for my sins and walk with confidence, knowing that I am in right standing with You. I am redeemed from the curse of sin and death by the blood of Jesus, and I live free from condemnation. I declare that I am a new creation. Old things in my life have passed away, and all things have become new. Help me to accomplish all You have for me to do as I wait excitedly for Your return. In Jesus's name, amen.

Keep to a Correct Course

Are You not from everlasting, O Lord my God, my Holy One? We shall not die. O Lord, You have appointed them for judgment; O Rock, You have marked them for correction.
—Habakkuk 1:12

Satan would inch us off the track of our destiny so minutely and perhaps unnoticeably that over time getting back to fulfilling our God-given purpose will seem monumental because of the mistakes we have made. However, if we correct course each day and keep our hearts open to God's correction in each moment, we can stay on track. Resisting temptation is not to deny living or the joys of life, as the devil would have us believe. It is disciplining ourselves to win the race God has called us to win. And sometimes it is not so much about the things we don't do, but more about keeping busy doing the things we should do.

Father, I seek today to be holy even as You are holy. Shine the light of Your Holy Spirit on any hidden sin I need to address. Let me walk in such brokenness and sensitivity to Your Spirit that I confess any and all sin before it takes root in my life. Keep my life on course, and never let me compromise or settle for anything less than Your best for me. Set my feet firmly on the path of righteousness. In the name of Jesus, amen.

August 31

Travel Lightly

Do you not know that those who run in a race all run, but one receives the prize? Run in such a way that you may obtain it.
—1 Corinthians 9:24

No runner getting ready for a marathon would fasten heavy diver's weights around his ankles as he prepares to start his race. Nor does he put on heavy blue jeans and a thick, winter jacket. Instead he dresses as lightly and sleekly as he can, ready to run for hours without stopping. In our lives as Christians called to dismantle the kingdom of darkness and establish the kingdom of light, we need to prepare ourselves and train for the marathons God has set before us—and not just for the short sprints we would prefer to run and be done with.

Father, take authority over my day and declare that I will run this race with confidence. I am equipped to achieve my goals and obtain the prize of the high calling of Jesus Christ in my life. I command this day to fully cooperate with me, and I call upon all of the resources of heaven that You have set aside for me to accomplish Your divine purpose and plan in my life today. I will not tire, trip, or fall. I will not merely survive, but thrive. I will finish well. In Jesus's name, amen.

September

September 1

Training Begins in Obscurity

Blessed be the Lord my Rock, who trains my hands for war, and my fingers for battle.
—Psalm 144:1

Thousands may gather in the arena to watch the end of a marathon and cheer on the participants, but training begins in obscurity. No one is around when the runners rise at 5:00 a.m. to get in a five-mile run before breakfast. In the same way, the crowds don't gather as we get up earlier than normal to have more time for prayer, Bible reading, and listening in on the big conversation of God's plans and directives for the day. This is the place we prepare for the race God has called us to, lightening the load by stripping away the bad habits and weaknesses that would trip us up, and putting on the love and grace that will strengthen us throughout the day.

Father, I rise early to meet with You. Your will is my assignment. I run this race to win the prize. I take no shortcuts in my preparation. I declare that I am strong in the Lord and in the power of His might. I have all I need for life and godliness. Father, let Your Word inspire me to righteousness. Without You I could do nothing, so I seek You first, and everything I need to fulfill Your purposes will be added to me. In Jesus's name, amen.

September 2

Be Prepared

Let us run with endurance that race that is set before us, looking unto Jesus, the author and finisher of our faith.
—Hebrews 12:1–2

We are meant to grow in maturity, wisdom, and endurance to be able to handle whatever the race of faith might throw at us, and to recommit ourselves to the author and finisher of our faith, the Alpha and Omega of our race. We must prepare today when the pressures on us are light so we will be able to face the tougher legs of the race with grace and courage. Overcomers are not born; they are developed over time, and prayer is the place that development takes place.

Father, the race isn't given to the swift or the strong but to the one who endures to the end. I recommit to fervently seek You in prayer. When I wait on You in prayer, You renew my strength. When I listen to You in prayer, You reveal Your secrets. I will choose to spend time with You each day, because that is where You equip me to finish this race. In the name of Jesus, amen.

September 3

Live by the Spirit

Man shall not live by bread alone, but by every word that proceeds from the mouth of God.
—Matthew 4:4

We are not spiritual beings by default; we must choose to live by the Spirit rather than be ruled by the things our physical senses and desires tell us we need. We can do this by fasting, just as Jesus did when He went into the wilderness before He began His ministry. This is disciplining the body to be in obedience to the Spirit in all things.

Father, I want to be led only by Your Spirit and not by the flesh. Strip away everything in me that is not like You. Anything that I listen to instead of or in addition to You must go in the name of Jesus. Anything I seek more than I seek You must be removed in the name of Jesus. I give You my whole heart and my full attention. Let my life be characterized by the fruit of Your Spirit. Let no evil way be found in me. In Jesus's name, amen.

September 4

Prayer Refines You

For you, O God, have tested us; You have refined us as silver is refined.
—Psalm 66:10

Prayer is not just a place of laying our petitions before heaven and lifting up God's holy name in praise and worship. It is also a place of being refined and broken and remolded. It is where we come before the Lord to be pruned of the habits, desires, and ambitions that would hinder all God has for us. It is the furnace where the impurities are refined out of the gold of our lives.

Father, I release You to move in my life. Transform my heart and mind. I welcome Your refining fire so that my heart may be as pure as gold. Let every bit of lukewarmness be replaced with the fire and zeal of God. You are a consuming fire, Lord. Consume me. Fill every inch of my heart, and burn away anything that would keep me from experiencing all You have for me. In Jesus's name, amen.

September 5

How Might You Fast?

When you fast, anoint your head and wash your face, so that you do not appear to men to be fasting, but to your Father, who is in the secret place; and your Father who sees in secret will reward you openly.
—Matthew 6:17–18

If your first thought in kneeling down to pray is that you need to go get something to eat before you start, check your e-mails, or look up something on the Internet, then you may have struck upon the very thing you should fast for a few days or a few weeks. Replace the time you would have spent on that activity with prayer. Then see what happens. I believe that as you do this, your faith will be renewed. You will find your "first love" for God being rejuvenated, and you will step further into the life God has been trying to give you since you first gave Him your heart. It will begin stretching what you can trust God for and what you can accomplish in Him.

Father, I decree and declare that I will look to You and You alone. I will not give in to the distractions all around me. Show me anything I have been putting above You; I will give it up. Show me anything that I have come to depend on more than You; I surrender it to You. You deserve my singular focus. In Jesus's name, amen.

Keep Reaching

Not that I have already attained, or am already perfected; but I press on, that I may lay hold of that for which Christ Jesus has also laid hold of me.
—Philippians 3:12

The "stretch" of faith in our lives should never really change. As we grow in God, so should the capacity of what we can accomplish in Christ. As our faith grows, so should the magnitude of our dreams and what we are asking God to do. In this way our faith is constantly reaching out for things that are just beyond our natural ability to gasp them.

Father, stretch my faith so that I can press forward into all You have prepared for me. Enlarge my territory. Empower me to lay hold of everything for which You laid hold of me. Deposit Your dreams and visions within my heart and renew my passion for the dreams You already revealed to me. In the name of Jesus I decree and declare that today I will make huge strides toward the dreams You have implanted in me. I see no impossibilities, only more chances for You to show Your strength and glory on my behalf. In the name of Jesus, amen.

September 7

Stretch After God

The gifts and the calling of God are irrevocable.
—Romans 11:29

There is a problem when we settle into the comfort zone of our gifts and purpose. When God calls us, He also supernaturally equips us with spiritual abilities in line with that divine mission and assignment. Regardless of whether we pursue God's glory in that purpose or our own, those divine gifts and abilities will still function in our lives. Thus it is possible to do great things and even see miracles happen in our ministries yet miss God by never continuing to stretch after Him.

Father, don't let me miss Your true purpose for my life. I release You to stretch me so I fulfill my calling. Even though it may not be pleasant, I know it will make me more fruitful for Your kingdom. In the name of Jesus I bind every spirit of fear and lukewarmness; I will not be satisfied with the status quo. I want all You have for me. I resist and repel all destiny-altering activities in the name of Jesus. I decree and declare that I will walk according to Your original plan and purpose for my life. In the name of Jesus, amen.

Does God Know You?

Many will say to Me in that day, "Lord, Lord, have we not prophesied in Your name, cast out demons in Your name, and done many wonders in Your name?" And then I will declare to them, "I never knew you; depart from Me, you who practice lawlessness!"
—Matthew 7:22–23

"I never *knew* you." Can you imagine what it would be like to hear those words when you finally get to meet Jesus face-to-face? But this is the outcome we risk if we try to do the will of God without seeking the face of God—if we settle into the comfortable pattern of doing the work of the Lord without getting our daily instructions from the Lord of the work. This is to inch our way off the path God has set before us without ever realizing it. It is to despise the greatness of what God wants to do through us for the compromise of living well enough as we are, for settling into a life without growth.

Father, I will not attempt to do Your will without first getting Your word on the matter. What You want to do in my life is too big for me to manage on my own. I can't even comprehend all You have prepared for me, so I certainly can't get to the finish line on my own. I need You! Father, order my steps according to Your Word. In Jesus's name, amen.

September 9

Focus on the Will of God

Do not lead us into temptation, but deliver us from the evil one.
—Matthew 6:13

Praying daily not to be led into temptation and to be delivered from evil is to center each day in the will of God and focus on the good you will do—the step-by-step righting of evil in our world without slipping back into old habits or complacent attitudes. Circumstances can bring setbacks, but with God, what the devil meant for evil will be turned on its head into good. We must open our ears to hear what needs to be covered in prayer for the protection of ourselves, our families, those within our realm of influence, and the missions to which God has assigned us and our churches.

Father, I declare that this day is pregnant with Your purposes. Open my heart and mind to receive Your direction. Show me what I need to cover in prayer today. Father, strengthen the hedge of protection around my life; my possessions; my family, friends, and associates; and my ministry. In the name of Jesus I will not be complacent or return to old ways; I will move boldly forward. As I focus on following Your will, I decree and declare that everything meant to harm me shall be turned around for my good. In the name of Jesus, amen.

Protect Yourself With God's Armor

Be strong in the Lord and in the power of his might. Put on the whole armor of God, that you may be able to stand against the wiles of the devil.
—Ephesians 6:10–11

If every day we are following God closely, then we are becoming dangerous to evil, and evil will want to become dangerous to us. However, if we stay clothed in the armor of Christ, we are protected. We man our posts, follow our orders, and thus keep temptations from tripping us up or selfishness from entering our hearts and sending us off course. It is the only way to triumph in the mission and purpose God has called us to—and to one day hear, "Well done, My good and faithful steward."

Father, I clothe myself in Your full armor today that I may be able to stand against the wiles of the devil. Guard me against seduction, temptation, and compromise. Sanctify my heart with Your word so that I don't stray. In the name of Jesus I decree and declare that I will triumph in the mission You have assigned to me. I will finish my course, and by Your grace I will hear You say, "Well done." In the name of Jesus, amen.

September 11

Establish the Kingdom

Your kingdom come. Your will be done on earth as it is in heaven.
—Matthew 6:10

How much are you willing to lay on the line that God's kingdom might be manifest in your midst? It is one thing to preach the gospel in our congregations and see people come to know Jesus; it is quite another to bring salvation in its every aspect to our neighborhoods and communities. To truly establish the kingdom of God on the earth is likely to take concentrated lifetimes; however, if we will apply the diligence of a William Wilberforce or a Dr. King, God will let us see victories—major victories—in our lifetimes. Are we willing to pay the price in time spent in prayer to see these things happen? Will we do today what is necessary for our children to live in a better tomorrow?

Father, I commit to pay the price to see transformation in the earth. By the authority I have through the blood of Jesus, I call for peace instead of crime and violence; economic growth instead of lack; servant leaders instead of the greedy and corrupt. Father, fill the atmosphere over my community and nation with Your glory and make it conducive to economic empowerment and spiritual renewal. Let Your kingdom come and Your will be done. In the name of Jesus, amen.

Take Hold of Salvation

Most assuredly, I say to you, unless one is born of water and the Spirit, he cannot enter the kingdom of God.
—John 3:5

In a world often filled with corruption and hatred, we have a great deal of work to do for God's will to be available to all. The call for social justice as well as a renewed transformational empowerment of the gospel message is crucial for the course correction needed. Certainly we must hold forth the full gospel of Jesus Christ and the power of what He did on the cross as the doorway to the kingdom of God. But is it enough for people to just stumble across the portal and *see* the kingdom of heaven? Should we not also take hold of all that salvation means and *enter* into it as well?

Father, use me to bring Your kingdom in the earth. Show me the cause that I am assigned to champion. Let me bear the light of Your glory and Your truth so that people may see it and find the way to You. Father, heal the land. Bring renewal and restoration. Empower the body of Christ to live true to our core values and the principles of Christ. I commit to do my part by taking a stand against violence, crime, and social injustice. Use me to orchestrate a divine course correction. In the name of Jesus, amen.

September 13

What Vision Have You Received?

Surely the Lord God does nothing, unless He reveals His secret to His servants the prophets.
—Amos 3:7

It will take the daily prayers of dedicated Christians everywhere for the body of Christ to become the catalyst for positive change Jesus has called it to be. It is from the manifested "bubbles" of God's presence, which are invited to the earth through prayer, that the kingdom of God becomes evident within our lives to touch the lives of others. Those manifestations of His presence are where we receive vision from heaven of how things should be. And as we meditate on the things God downloads into our spirits, His divine strategies, wisdom, and inner resolve grow in our lives. These enable us to walk out His plans on the earth for accomplishing His purpose and calling for our lives.

Father, as I spend time in prayer today, download into my spirit Your divine strategies and wisdom. Cause my resolve to grow, enabling me to walk out Your plans in the earth. I welcome Your presence into my day. Let it be with me, before me, behind me, in me, beneath me, above me, on my right, and on my left. As I yield to Your plans and purposes for this day, use me to touch others' lives. In the name of Jesus, amen.

What Is Your Fruit Like?

You will know them by their fruits.... Every good tree bears good fruit, but a bad tree bears bad fruit.
—Matthew 7:16–17

It is one thing to *hear* from heaven, but will we *do* what it takes to walk out our mission and assignments each and every day? Jesus never said that we would be judged by what we say we believe, but by the fruits of the actions dictated by what we truly do believe. From discipline and wise strategy come victory, both on the battlefield and in the overall war. If we are properly plugging into prayer and hearing God's voice in relation to each day, we are plugging into the kingdom, power, and glory that are forever God's alone.

Father, I seek You today because You are my power source. It's not enough for me to declare Your words over my day. Empower me to align my actions with what I confess. I reject and repel all unbelief in the name of Jesus. In the name of Jesus I command my mind and my heart to come into agreement with what You're saying about my life and future. I break every mental barrier that would keep me from accepting Your truth. I decree and declare that I will be known by the good fruit You chose for me to bring forth. In the name of Jesus, amen.

September 15

See What God Sees

Then as I looked, I saw a door standing open in heaven, and the same voice I had heard before spoke to me like a trumpet blast. The voice said, "Come up here, and I will show you what must happen after this."
—Revelation 4:1, NLT

God consciousness and spiritual sight are required to pray from God's perspective. You must see situations and people as God sees them, or else your prayers may actually be working against God's designs rather than in accordance with them. You want to stay seated in the heavenly realm—in Christ—so that you can attest to the movements of the adversary and stand in the gap for those who are yet to understand the true nature of the things of the Spirit. When you can see the landscape and territories as God sees them, when you can see the strategic layout of God's plan, then your prayers take on a potency and intensity that annihilate satanic entrenchments.

Father, You have seated me in heavenly places in Christ. Give me a fresh revelation of who I am in You and the incredible access I have as Your child. You are the only great and awesome God, and I ask humbly that You open my spiritual eyes to see things from Your perspective that I might pray with prophetic precision and annihilate the strongholds of the enemy. In the name of Jesus, amen.

Grow in Your Senses

When you look at a baby, it's just that: a body you can look at and touch. But the person who takes shape within is formed by something you can't see and touch—the Spirit—and becomes a living spirit.
—John 3:6, The Message

When we are born again, we suddenly have a complete new set of senses—senses that perceive in the Spirit realm the same way our natural senses perceive in the physical realm. However, while we don't remember how difficult it was to learn to use our senses as we grew from babies to toddlers and into small children, as Christians we too often balk at these same difficulties as we try to understand the things we perceive spiritually. Like the man Jesus healed from blindness who first saw "men like trees, walking" (Mark 8:24), we need an additional touch of Christ or more experience learning to see before we really understand the overwhelming nature of perceiving and understanding spiritual things.

Father, I welcome another touch from You so that I can gain greater understanding of the things of the spirit. Sharpen my spiritual senses to hear Your words, taste Your goodness, feel Your presence, smell Your aroma, and see Your glory. Remove anything that would keep me from growing in my knowledge of You. In the name of Jesus, amen.

September 17

YOU CANNOT DO IT ALONE

For flesh and blood has not revealed this to you, but My Father who is in heaven.
—MATTHEW 16:17

In order to pray and war for our communities according to heaven's strategies, we must come to grips with the fact that there is no victory to be gained or territory to be taken that will ever be of our doing alone. We cannot beat the devil, but Christ has already defeated him. It is not the clever advertising of our churches, the efficiency of our programs, or the charisma of our preachers that saves souls. It is the revelation of Jesus for who He is and what He has done. That revelation does not come from other people, but rather from the Father. Effective prayer is not, then, a matter of beating demons as much as it is revealing Christ. What better way is there to pray than praying the same prayers Jesus is praying as He intercedes at the right hand of the Father?

Father, give me a deeper revelation of who I am in Christ and the authority I have in Him. Sharpen my sensitivity to tune in to heaven and align my prayers with those of Jesus, the Great Intercessor. I thank You, Lord, that because Christ defeated Satan on the cross, I war from a place of victory when I decree Your will and word over my life. In the name of Jesus, amen.

Take the Battle to the Enemy

The vision is yet for an appointed time; but at the end it will speak, and it will not lie.
—Habakkuk 2:3

This is the final stage of prayer that few seem to reach: when we can move from our daily defensive prayers for protection to taking the battle to the enemy as God directs us. This is the realm of prayer engaged by champions and true heroes of faith about which few hear. We often know the names of the preachers and evangelists, but we do not know the names of all those who paved the way in the Spirit to have the results they did. These did not seek the spotlight, only the continual presence of God. Having covered things defensively in their prayers, they were awarded the privilege of standing at the war table in the center of God's strategic, high-command center and learning God's plans for the earth, and then they were allowed to take part in seeing them come to pass.

Father, take me into new spiritual dimensions that I may be among those who stand at Your heavenly war table, learn Your plans, and strategically release Your will into the earth. Prepare my heart for the responsibility of this place in the spirit. I ask that You empower me to pray defensively and to see true transformation as a result. In the name of Jesus, amen.

September 19

Is the Enemy Scouting You?

Be sober, be vigilant; because your adversary the devil walks about like a roaring lion, seeking whom he may devour.
—1 Peter 5:8

Satan desires to ambush our souls to cause us to be afraid. His only chance of victory is to keep us from praying, and if he can't do that, then he wants to keep our prayers short and ineffective. He pulls out his weapons of temptation, accusation, deception, and empty hopes so we will cower in the corner and not enter the fray. He wants to keep us downcast, discouraged, and doubting the importance of prayer. However, our fight in prayer has no boundaries. As the Word of God takes up residence in us, there is no doubt it has the power to transform the way we see the world. It becomes clear that the best tactics of the enemy are to convince us we should not answer the bell for the next round of the fight.

Father, as I study Your Word, give me a deeper revelation of Your truth. Let it take root deep in my heart and transform the way I think. Let me never lose sight of who I am in You. In You I am victorious over the enemy. I decree and declare that I will not fall into Satan's trap, but I will stay faithful in prayer until the battle is won. In the name of Jesus, amen.

Pray Fearlessly

Be anxious for nothing, but in everything by prayer and supplication, with thanksgiving, let your requests be made known to God.
—Philippians 4:6

You must pray fearlessly and relentlessly, knowing it is God who wars on your behalf—it is God who teaches your hands to war, and it is God to whom the ultimate victory will go. You can pray fearlessly because you have nothing to lose. Everything you have belongs to God and will return to Him. He is Lord of all and is worthy of a people who trust Him implicitly and will fight without fear. This is the realm of prayer that changes things on the earth, the place where you have so much faith in God that nothing—even the fear of death on the battlefield to which you are called—can keep you from your God-given mission. You become like Paul, taking the fight to the gates of hell rather than standing at your own gate and praying the devil can't get in.

Father, I declare that I am fearless in battle, knowing that You war on my behalf. As I pray relentlessly, I expect the situation to change for the better. I give everything to You for the sake of the calling on my life. I have nothing to lose, so I will pray without fear. I trust You completely. In the name of Jesus, amen.

September 21

Be Brave in Faith

Have I not commanded you? Be strong and of good courage; do not be afraid, nor be dismayed, for the Lord *your God is with you wherever you go.*
—Joshua 1:9

In any new venture or stance that is righteous, great faith is required—and great faith is always accompanied by action. The hindrance to obedience to the call of God is when faith is challenged by fear in such a way that the believer is paralyzed and does nothing. The cowardly will not be seen in heaven (Rev. 21:8). Why? Because if we fear, we don't have the love of God in us, for His "perfect love casts out fear" (1 John 4:18).

Thank You, Lord, for Your perfect love that casts out fear. I decree and declare that I am strong and of good courage. I do not fear the giants in my land of promise. I do not think my problems are bigger than You. I stand in faith, always ready to obey Your Word, because I know You are with me wherever I go. In the name of Jesus, amen.

September 22

Overcome Fear With Love

In Christ, neither our most conscientious religion nor disregard of religion amounts to anything. What matters is something far more interior: faith expressed in love.
—Galatians 5:6, The Message

In order to move in faith, the love of God must be seated in our consciousness. We have to know and experience the unfailing love of God. Our courage, then, does not show that we don't have fear, but that we have assessed the situation and deem the Word of God to be of greater impact. Fear of the Lord is not something that should make us afraid before Him but something that should deliver us from being afraid of anything else. If we have truly experienced God's presence, then what on earth could ever make us afraid to do as He has instructed us?

Father, sharpen my awareness of Your presence and power today. Let me know and experience Your love in a deeper way so I will not give in to fear. You are the only great and awesome God. Nothing I will face today or any day is bigger than You are. I trust Your Word and believe that You give me power to overcome. Seat Your unfailing love in my consciousness and saturate my heart with a holy fear of You. I decree and declare that I will fear only You. I will not be afraid to follow Your instructions. In the name of Jesus, amen.

September 23

Pray Courageously

They overcame him by the blood of the Lamb and by the word of their testimony, and they did not love their lives to the death.
—Revelation 12:11

Because we pray and know how to find God in prayer, we have courage, and we pray courageously. We do not fear praying for things that are impossible with man, because His love has cast out fear and permitted us to participate in His overcoming of the world.

Thank You, Father, for Your perfect love that casts out fear. Because You loved me enough to die on the cross, making me more than a conqueror, I can participate in Your overcoming of the world. What is impossible with man is easy for You. I come before You boldly in prayer because You have overcome the world, and You are certainly more than able to handle anything that comes my way today. Thank You for being so faithful to me. In the name of Jesus, amen.

September 24

Be Prepared for Battle

What king, going to make war against another king, does not sit down first and consider whether he is able with ten thousand to meet him who comes against him with twenty thousand?
—Luke 14:31

Taking the fight to the gates of the enemy is not the work of a novice. There is a trust and authority that must be earned in a steadfast dedication to prayer. I know there are many who will want to practice living it before all of the others, but it won't work that way. A novice doesn't have the necessary wisdom because he or she lacks the necessary experience and training. That is why the Scriptures warn about putting a novice in spiritual leadership too quickly. We must count the cost before we engage in the fight.

Father, help me to continually grow in You. I submit myself to Your boot camp so I will not be a novice in battle, but fully mature and trained by Your Word and Your Spirit to be ready for war. I decree and declare that I remain steadfast in prayer and steadily move from glory to glory and faith to faith. In the name of Jesus, amen.

September 25

Take Hold of Wisdom

Happy is the man who finds wisdom, and the man who gains understanding; for her proceeds are better than the profits of silver, and her gain than fine gold.
—Proverbs 3:13–14

No one has to remain ignorant or unwise. The Book of Proverbs gives direction, and Scripture gives the power to take hold of wisdom. Wisdom is the marriage of understanding the protocols of the heavenly realm and the knowledge of the appropriate response in the earthly realm. One comes through study of the Word, the other through experience and revelation. Both take time.

Father, Your Word says that if anyone lacks wisdom, he should ask You. So I ask You for wisdom. Open my eyes and ears to the things of the spirit and protect me from spiritual blindness and deafness. Teach me the protocols of heaven and give me divine understanding of the times and seasons so I will know exactly how to pray. Enlighten the eyes of my understanding, Father, that I may grow in You. In the name of Jesus, amen.

Pray Wisely

Wisdom is better than weapons of war.
—Ecclesiastes 9:18

When you pray wisely, you will always pray according to the principles of the Word of God you have learned. Wisdom is powerful. The wisdom of God supersedes the cleverness loaded into the wisdom of human beings. When you pray wisely, you pray in agreement with the Word of God and can accomplish more in one breath than many who spend years cleverly maneuvering to get what they want. To do this, you must pray the Word, not your worries. Load the Word in your heart and transform your mouth into a semiautomatic weapon of precision, speaking only that which agrees with God. What you speak must show that you know God well enough that you can be confident in taking Him at His Word.

Father, I declare that I am wise and therefore pray in accordance with Your Word. I do not rely on my own strength or understanding because that is what those who are foolish do. I pray Your Word, not my worries. I hide Your Word in my heart, Lord. Let it change my thoughts and speech so my words are always aligned with what is in Scripture and what is being said in heaven. Because I take You completely at Your Word, I will not be put to shame. In the name of Jesus, amen.

September 27

Grow in Knowing God

And this is eternal life, that they know you the only true God, and Jesus Christ whom you have sent.
—John 17:3, esv

When you read and mediate on God's Word prayerfully, it becomes like reading letters written personally to you. Like with a close friend, after a while you start to complete each other's sentences and know exactly what the other means even when they can't express it themselves. There are things you will come to know about the Father that no one will succeed at convincing you of otherwise. You gain a knowledge of Him that God has chosen specifically to reveal to you. Then when you make petitions in prayer, you have a distinct advantage, because you've learned the particular nuances of how to ask in order to appeal to His likes and dislikes. You pray knowledgeably—you simply agree in prayer with God, praying the same prayers Jesus is praying as He intercedes for the earth. Can there be a more powerful prayer of agreement than that?

Father, draw me closer to You today. Purify my heart with Your Word. Reveal Yourself to me in a deeper way. Bring my words and thoughts in alignment with Your words and thoughts so that my prayers are in sync with the intercession being made in heaven. In the name of Jesus, amen.

Drop the Agenda

And you shall know the truth, and the truth shall make you free.
—John 8:32

Knowing the truth and knowing yourself truly help you to drop façades and look to God for His divine purpose instead of being fooled by your own hidden agendas. This allows you to pray the heart of God, praying prophetically as He gives you the words to unlock the barriers keeping His will from the earth.

Father, like Paul I desire to know You and the power of Your resurrection and the fellowship of Your suffering that I may become more like You. Free me of false pretenses through the knowledge of Your Word, and increase my knowledge of who I am in You. Cleanse my heart of my own agenda. Break down every barrier in my life that would keep me from hearing clearly from You. Bring everything that is misaligned into divine alignment today so that my words and actions work to advance only Your kingdom agenda. In the name of Jesus, amen.

September 29

Partake in the Exploits of God

This charge I commit to you, son Timothy, according to the prophecies previously made concerning you, that by them you may wage the good warfare.
—1 Timothy 1:18

In praying God's words as well as His Word, we tap into the genius of God and legislate His oracles into the earth realm. It is God who has set the stage for our progression into His image and likeness, and it will be God who watches over His words to perform them. The people who speak out of the Spirit of God will do great exploits in His name. To do so means to come into agreement with the God-breathed words spoken in the law and the prophets, as well as individualized words of direction revealed and received through our spirits from God. As consummate planners and strategists, we must follow every word that proceeds out of God's mouth and pray prophetically, just as Paul advised Timothy to do.

Father, I live off every word that proceeds out of Your mouth. They nourish my spirit and change my perspective. I open my heart to receive fresh revelation from You today. I come into agreement with the words You've spoken to me; they will come to pass, because You watch over Your word to perform it. I commit to speak out of Your Spirit and not of myself so I can do great exploits in Your name. In Jesus's name, amen.

Escape Unscathed

Then Shadrach, Meshach, and Abed-Nego came from the midst of the fire...[and] the hair of their head was not singed nor were their garments affected, and the smell of fire was not on them.
—Daniel 3:26–27

The enemy of your soul stands in amazement when he hurls his most destructive mechanisms and a simple tactic from the Lord makes it look as though you have never been in the fire or flood Satan intended for you. You walk away looking good and smelling good, and the kingdom of darkness is left defeated and befuddled. Just like Shadrach, Meshach, and Abednego, you walk out rejoicing in the power of your Savior.

I praise You today for all the times You've brought me through situations that seemed hopeless. Thank You for all the times You've turned situations completely around. When I was in sin, You cleansed me and made me new. When I deserved punishment, You showed me grace and gave me what I didn't deserve. I stand in awe of You, God. I decree that the works of the devil are destroyed and the plans and purpose of God shall prevail. I declare that I am advancing the cause of Christ in every region. I am promoting the King and proclaim that His kingdom is here. In the name of Jesus, amen.

October

October 1

Stay Relentless

We are not of those who shrink back and are destroyed, but of those who have faith and preserve their souls.
—Hebrews 10:39, esv

You will obtain a tenacity of spirit when you stay vigilantly and relentlessly focused on seeking God in prayer. Look intently to the matters God has exposed in the realm of the Spirit. Pray with force and perseverance. Once your focus is locked, the intensity of prayer should escalate until it dismantles the illegal movements of the satanic kingdom. The term *vigilant* connotes a stare or gaze that defies anything to move out of timing or order. It is a privilege to move with this kind of intensity in undistracted and undeterred prayer.

In the name of Jesus, I declare that I pray with vigilance. I do not move out of the timing of God, and my prayers are unhindered and undistracted because of the power of the blood of Jesus. Father, I seek You relentlessly. Open my eyes and ears to experience supernatural and miraculous realms. I break through that which is insurmountable and impenetrable into the realm of the miraculous. I decree and declare that I am not lukewarm, but I have a tenacious spirit as a kingdom warrior. In the name of Jesus, amen.

Review Your Options

Therefore we do not lose heart. Even though our outward man is perishing, yet the inward man is being renewed day by day.
—2 Corinthians 4:16

In every situation it is best to review the possible outcomes before you begin to choose your course of action. You must know yourself, your own faith, what God has promised, and what His will is for any given circumstances. You cannot afford to be impetuous and get ahead of God. You must heed the intelligence that comes from the throne room of heaven. Without it, you cannot understand what is happening and will lose heart.

Father, I will not get ahead of You today. I will listen for the intelligence that comes from Your throne room so that my prayers are strategic and prophetically aligned to bring breakthrough. I decree and declare that I do not lose heart in prayer because I wait for Your instructions and do not follow my own plans. In the name of Jesus, amen.

October 3

What If...?

Remember the former things long past, for I am God, and there is no other; I am God, and there is no one like Me, declaring the end from the beginning, and from the ancient times things which have not been done, saying, "My purpose will be established, and I will accomplish all My good pleasure."

—Isaiah 46:9–10, nas

What happens if God decides not to move as you expect or has a different timetable? What if God realigns your life such that you will not have any crutch but Him? Can it be possible that God will accomplish the words He has spoken to you or about you in a different manner than you have imagined? No matter what the answers are, you have to look at the end from the beginning and come out with an answer that agrees with kingdom mandates. None of this can really be done until you are practiced in the art of spiritual knowing, something that only comes through praying until you get the answer.

Father, I press in to You today for the answers I seek. I welcome Your response, even if it is different from what I expected. I trust You to fulfill Your promises to me in whatever manner You see fit. I wait patiently for Your timing. In the name of Jesus, amen.

God's Word Will Not Return Void

Now go, write it on a tablet before them and inscribe it on a scroll, that it may serve in the time to come as a witness forever.
—Isaiah 30:8, nas

If God promised it, you can expect it to come to pass, but the how is up to God and can only be discovered if you ask. When you come to Him with such prayers, don't let your mind wander or wonder. Keep in the forefront of your focus the things God has embedded and inscribed on your heart. Whatever you have heard from God or read in His Word that touched your spirit and ignited your soul, that word spoken to you shall not return to God without producing results. God made great and precious promises, and they shall come to pass.

Father, I stand in faith today believing that the prophetic words You have spoken to me will come to pass in their correct season. I know Your words will not return to You void; they will accomplish that for which they have been sent. I call forth every promise that I let die because of doubt and unbelief. In the name of Jesus I command you to live. I decree and declare that every word shall come to pass and produce a great harvest for Your kingdom. In the name of Jesus, amen.

October 5

God Has Assigned It

For He performs what is appointed for me, and many such decrees are with Him.
—Job 23:14, NAS

The spirit realm is the causal realm, so expect that whatever you are praying shall come to pass once you know it has been sealed in the Spirit. God has already released these things before the foundations of the earth. He has assigned a specific time and season for them to come to pass. Do not be counterproductive in your prayers by praying one thing and confessing another. Be consistent in knowing that whatever you commit to releasing that pertains to your life will be loosed—positive or negative, in faith or in unbelief—and whatsoever you bind is bound. Do you understand? The Bible says whatsoever—good or bad, little or big—it will come to pass.

In the name of Jesus I decree that I discipline my mouth so that I speak words of faith and loose only the plans and purposes of God in my life. I will not undermine my intercession by praying one thing and confessing another. I decree that there will be synergy between what I say in prayer and what I say throughout my day. I declare that nothing shall prevent God's Word from bearing fruit in my life. In Jesus's name, amen.

Let the Spirit Teach You

Meanwhile, the moment we get tired in the waiting, God's Spirit is right alongside helping us along. If we don't know how or what to pray, it doesn't matter. He does our praying in and for us, making prayer out of our wordless sighs, our aching groans.
—Romans 8:26–27, The Message

When it is said that we are to pray in the Spirit, the dynamic we are really looking to gain is alignment with the rhythm and mind of God. As we seek this, the Spirit of the Lord teaches us how to pray. He speaks to our hearts to cause us to embrace the protocols of heaven and helps us daily take the small steps that put us in agreement with heaven. Praying in the Spirit in this way acknowledges there is much heaven has to impart to us. Sometimes we do not know what to pray or how to pray, and so the Spirit of God assists us in our inability.

Father, cause my prayers to align with the rhythm and mind of God. Teach me to pray in the Spirit. Speak to my heart and show me how I ought to pray. Educate me in the protocols of heaven. I decree that I stand in agreement with Your words and will see Your will manifest in my life. In the name of Jesus, amen.

It's About Deliverance

The gates of hell shall not prevail against [My church].
—Matthew 16:18, kjv

Our ultimate responsibility is not to be defensive and protective of what we have but to be offensive that His kingdom might break beyond the gates of hell itself—or at least into the brothels of Bangkok, the slave-filled tin mines of the Congo, the kidnappers of invisible children in Darfur, the meth labs in your city, or whatever other hole Satan has trapped human beings in that he might slowly suck away their souls. We make a mistake if we think God cannot reach into these places and bring deliverance, but we also make a mistake if we think it is all up to His sovereignty. We must invite Him into our world in order for Him to change things, and we must battle in the heavenlies until His answers make their way to the earth.

Because nothing is too hard for You, God, I expect my prayers to bring results. I do battle in the heavenlies for breakthrough on earth. I decree that everything the enemy has swallowed up must be coughed up and released. My family, my finances, my community—they must be loosed and released in the name of Jesus. I decree and declare that nothing will be held back. I will see transformation as I persevere in prayer. In the name of Jesus, amen.

Have Integrity in Prayer

When you pray, you shall not be like the hypocrites. For they love to pray standing in the synagogues and on the corners of the streets, that they may be seen by men. Assuredly, I say to you, they have their reward.
—Matthew 6:5–6

It doesn't matter how good you look to people at church or at work. It doesn't matter what your reputation in your community is or if you have a small fortune in the bank. It doesn't matter if you show up at every prayer meeting and spend every hour of your church's twenty-four-hour prayer vigil on your face before God weeping. The only way to have true integrity is if you have integrity in your personal prayer closet before God. It isn't about being seen by others or about what others think; it's about what God thinks and how much He trusts you with what He is doing on the earth.

Father, may I be known by You for my integrity—what I do in the secret place of prayer when no one is looking but You. My priority is not to be seen as righteous by men but to be seen as righteous by You. Create in me a clean heart, Lord, so that I can be trusted with Your strategic plans. I long to partner with You in advancing Your kingdom in the earth. In the name of Jesus, amen.

October 9

Put Prayer First

I love those who love me, and those who diligently seek me will find me.
—Proverbs 8:17

If you read the stories of the great generals of prayer of the past, you will begin to see some patterns. One of the most important is that they didn't fit in prayer around their schedule of activities and speaking engagements; they fit in their activities and engagements around their prayer times. As Stephen Covey advocates, you have to put the "big rocks"—the most important things—onto your calendar first, or all of the little distractions and "urgent" matters of your day will not leave room for doing what is important. Prayer—or more simply put, "meeting with our Lord"—must be first place in everything we do if we are to know His plan, be free of worldly and earthly burdens, and have His wisdom in every matter.

Father, meeting with You today is my priority. I do not pray in hopes of getting Your stamp of approval on my plans. I pray to get Your plan and then set my agenda around it. Nothing on my agenda today is more important than You. I take the time I need today to seek You. Spirit of God, I release You to direct my day according to Your agenda and calendar. In the name of Jesus, amen.

Stand at the Edge of Eternity

As you do not know what is the way of the wind, or how the bones grow in the womb of her who is with child, so you do not know the works of God who makes everything.
—Ecclesiastes 11:5

Unless we make it a priority, we will never get the downloads from heaven that we need to fulfill our purposes on the earth. That will likely mean spending a lot of time at the edge of eternity calling out into what feels like a void, banging on heaven's gate and feeling as if no one is home. But the way things seem and the way they actually are, are two different things.

Though it may seem that I bring the same requests to You, beating on heaven's door without response, I trust that You are working in ways I cannot comprehend. I stand on the edge of eternity, continuing to ask and continuing to knock, until change comes. Like a seed that splits and grows roots before its sprout can be seen above the soil, so are my prayers bringing forth fruit. I thank You, Father, that You are always working on my behalf. In the name of Jesus, amen.

October 11

Plant Thought Seeds

Now may He who supplies seed to the sower, and bread for food, supply and multiply the seed you have sown and increase the fruits of your righteousness.
—2 Corinthians 9:10

As in every seed, life-giving power resides in every spoken word. This principle illustrates how the spiritual law of incubation and manifestation works. Everything you see in the natural began as a spiritual seed—that is, as a thought. When you plant a seed in the ground, you do not know what is happening with it until it pushes through the soil. There will be days and even weeks you might think nothing is happening at all, but it is growing and sprouting and getting ready to bear fruit. Prayer is the same way. What we do in secret may even be secret from us for a time, but when it manifests and sprouts, God will be glorified in it before all men.

I thank You, Lord, that You are always working on my behalf, even when I can't see the results. I remain steadfast in prayer today, knowing that in due season I will reap. Bring about Your purposes in their correct time. I will wait patiently for You, knowing the answer is on its way. In the name of Jesus, amen.

Live by the Divine Nature

His divine power has given to us all things that pertain to life and godliness, through the knowledge of Him who called us by glory and virtue.
—2 Peter 1:3

Through the knowledge of God we will receive all things needed for life and godliness—god-like-ness, if you will. This is being more like Jesus, ushering more of the kingdom of heaven onto this earth, fighting for the same justice Christians throughout history have been fighting for in establishing each generation. We have exceedingly great and precious promises that have been given to us so that we can live by the divine nature God has put into everyone who believes Jesus died for his or her sins and was raised back to life—that we would live by the fullness of the Holy Spirit seeded into us as a down payment on all God plans to do in, through, and for us.

I declare that I have everything I need for life and godliness. Each day I am becoming more like Jesus, and each day more of Your kingdom is being released in the earth. I have exceedingly great and precious promises in You, and I decree that they will be released in their proper season. Because of Your power at work within me, I declare that I will do great exploits for my King and Your kingdom. In Jesus's name, amen.

October 13

Do You Need to Repent?

Remember therefore from where you have fallen; repent and do the first works.
—Revelation 2:5

There are times when we earnestly are in denial as to the truth of our situation or the circumstances surrounding others. Many times we blame the devil for our problems when in fact they are due to our own lack of diligence, discipline, courage, conviction, or character. The Spirit of truth, the Holy Spirit, is able to help us discern where we actually stand with God in such situations. Although God is always on our side, there are times when genuine repentance needs to take place before He can effectively address what is happening in our lives. God is not looking to bail people out who won't grow up and take responsibility, but He is quick to stand with those who desire to grow up enough that they can reach out and help others.

Spirit of God, I release You to search my heart today. See if there is any unrighteous way in me. If I have been praying amiss, if my motives have not been pure, or if I have fallen into sin, knowingly or unknowingly, I repent. I want nothing to separate me from You or hinder my prayers. I take full responsibility for my actions. Father, make me more like You. In the name of Jesus, amen.

Integrity Wins

Blessed are the pure in heart, for they shall see God.
—Matthew 5:8, esv

When the kingdom of heaven and the kingdom of this world clash, it will be those who have heard from heaven who will supply the strategies to victory. It will be those with the most integrous—pure, honest, sound, strong, untainted, and stable—prayer lives who arise with the answers and the conviction to see the fight to its proper finish.

Father, give me a pure heart before You, and remove any blockages that would prevent me from communicating with You. I lift up my voice like a trumpet in Zion to declare that You are Lord. You reign over my life. You destroy the works of the enemy. Pierce the darkness with the light of Your presence. In the name of Jesus, amen.

October 15

Hold Nothing Back

Draw near to God and He will draw near to you. Cleanse your hands, you sinners; and purify your hearts, you double-minded.... Humble yourselves in the sight of the Lord, and He will lift you up.

—James 4:8–10

God specializes in turning lives around—no matter where we start or how little influence we may have had before, He gives us power to transform the world around us if we will but encounter Him and give ourselves to Him without holding anything back. One person and God can form a majority. This shows how prayer not only changes us, but it also changes circumstances—and it not only changes circumstances, but it can also change hearts and minds for generations to come. The evil of a dictator or tyrant may reign for a few decades, but the good done by men and women of character and integrity influences centuries.

With You nothing shall be impossible for me. When You step on the scene, You bring complete transformation. Father, paralyze that which hinders me from moving into greatness. Roll the boulders away that are blocking my financial, social, physical, or spiritual breakthrough. Destroy every evil device, strategy, or technology fashioned for my failure. Through Christ I bulldoze my way past every barrier. In the name of Jesus, amen.

You Have Power

Behold, I give you the authority to trample on serpents and scorpions, and over all the power of the enemy, and nothing shall by any means hurt you.
—Luke 10:19

We indeed live in a time when there are horrible things happening on the earth, but we are not powerless to change those things for the better. We may balk at what we can accomplish because we do not have authority or access in the halls of national governments, but we forget that we have authority to influence decisions made in the council chambers of the very Creator of the universe Himself. We have influence. We are change agents. We have authority in the heavenlies. We are, in fact, the keys to making a difference for thousands if not millions. We do it through the atomic power of prayer.

Father, I declare that I am an agent of change in the earth. I use my influence to bring Your kingdom and make a difference in the world around me. I will walk boldly in my purpose today and every day, knowing that You have given me authority over the enemy. I decree and declare that nothing will hinder Your plans and purposes. Your kingdom will come, and Your will shall be done. In the name of Jesus, amen.

October 17

God Has Called You

Therefore we also pray always for you that our God would count you worthy of this calling.
—2 Thessalonians 1:11

It's time to turn our eyes away from our circumstances and to the God who called Joseph from the prison cell, Moses from the desert, David from the fields, Peter from his fishing boat, and Paul from his terrorism. Wherever you are in space and time is the place God has placed you to see what you see and be concerned about what you are concerned about. Chances are, what bothers you also bothers God. You are His agent. Wherever you are, make things different.

Through the authority I have in You to decree a thing and see it established, I speak to the spiritual, economic, social, and political climate around me and command it to shift now in the name of Jesus. I alter the environment around me and declare that it is now suitable for my ministry, my loved ones, my work, and my ideas to thrive. I establish a supernatural environment for miracles to occur. I decree that wherever I am, change happens. Let only Your will be done in and through me. In the name of Jesus, amen.

Prayer Is a Spiritual Force

Call to Me, and I will answer you, and show you great and mighty things, which you do not know.
—Jeremiah 33:3

Prayer is a kingdom technology and spiritual weapon of mass destruction against evil. In the natural, technology is the actual application of scientific methodologies, especially to systemic, industrial, or commercial objectives. Prayer is the application of heaven's methodologies that systematically brings to pass God's plan for man. Prayer is a spiritual force that exerts and exercises continuous and decisive influence on both the natural and spiritual worlds, effecting change within its systems and inhabitants. Therefore prayer should be the salient feature of every believer's life strategy. Without it, we are doomed. With it, we are more than a conqueror.

Thank You for being a God who hears and answers prayer. I stand today as more than a conqueror because of the power of the cross. I seek You daily in prayer, and I declare that Your plans will be made manifest in my life. I take the limits off my thinking and advance into new territory. I declare that Your kingdom agenda for my life, ministry, loved ones, workplace, community, and nation will be established because of the power of prayer. In Jesus's name, amen.

Where Are You?

Commit your work to the Lord, and
your plans will be established.
—Proverbs 16:3, esv

Where will you be when God comes to you with His greater plan for your life? Will you be open to step into it, or will you need to be schooled on the backside of the desert as Moses was? Will you need to go through a humbling process as rigorous as Joseph's? The difference will be determined by your prayer life—one way or the other.

Holy Spirit, I invite You to search my heart today to see if there is anything in me that is not like You. Cleanse me and renew a right spirit within me so that I don't resist what You desire to do in my life. I humble myself before You. I surrender my will and my way, knowing Your plans are always best. As I seek You daily in prayer, keep my heart right before You so I will not miss out on anything You want to bring into my life. In the name of Jesus, amen.

Called and Separated

Now separate to Me Barnabas and Saul for the work to which I have called them.
—Acts 13:2

We see two distinct events occurring in the lives of all Bible heroes—a point of calling and a point of launching into that calling, or what many have labeled being *called* and then *separated*. Paul had been called to the work of God since before he was born (Gal. 1:15)—but he would not be separated into that calling until God saw that he was ready to be the man capable of walking in that calling. We see there is always a time of preparation of which intimate, consistent prayer is a major component.

Father, prepare me for what You are calling me to in the school of prayer. I desire to influence the world around me for Your glory. I long to promote and proclaim Your majesty in the earth, so I submit to the training You are putting me through. I will not complain because I know it is all for my good. In prayer I grow close to You. I hear Your heart and I learn Your secrets and I discover how to pray through any circumstance until there is breakthrough. I will not try to sidestep this process. Rather, I thank You for allowing me to train with You and making me strong and bold for Your kingdom. In the name of Jesus, amen.

October 21

We Need Each Other

Now you are the body of Christ, and members individually.
—1 Corinthians 12:27

Without the body, Christ the head has no vehicle to put into action His thoughts, His concepts, His ideologies, His insights, His precepts, His philosophies, or His strategies. He prophetically speaks these things into the atmosphere of the church—into the "bubble" of His presence that is His body on the earth—looking for those who will listen and put His plans into operation. But each of us holds only a part of the "mystery" of God's plan for the earth. We need each other to get the whole picture. Thus the church is not a building; it is a collection of all those who hear and obey God's voice. It is the compilation and integration of all those who know how to pray, hear from heaven, and then look for ways to make what they hear a reality on the earth.

I am not alone in my efforts to bring Your will to pass on earth. I am part of a community of people around the world who are also demolishing strongholds and setting captives free through prayer. Because of the cross, our victory is sure. In the name of Jesus I declare and decree that even amid persecution the church shall grow. We shall rise up with boldness and advance Your kingdom. In the name of Jesus, amen.

Angels Are Watching Us

To the intent that now the manifold wisdom of God might be made known by the church to the principalities and powers in the heavenly places, according to the eternal purpose which He accomplished in Christ Jesus our Lord.
—Ephesians 3:10–12

Even the angels in heaven are waiting to understand the mystery of God's plan of the ages for our universe—and they won't learn it from going to God and asking. They can only learn it by watching the church on the earth and seeing God's mysterious plan revealed through us. As Paul stated earlier in Ephesians, God has "made known to us the mystery of His will, according to His good pleasure" (Eph. 1:9). That is quite a responsibility and quite a privilege at the same time. And somehow I think it is a whole lot more than just adding names to our list of people whose souls got saved through our ministries. God has bigger mysteries to reveal to the world. He still has "greater works" (John 14:12) to be done.

It is my privilege to be part of Your plans and to learn the mystery of Your will. Perform Your "greater works" through me. Train me in the school of prayer to fulfill the mission to which I have been called so that the earth will be filled with Your glory. In the name of Jesus, amen.

God's Embassies on Earth

Now I plead with you, brethren, by the name of our Lord Jesus Christ, that you all speak the same thing, and that there be no divisions among you, but that you be perfectly joined together in the same mind and in the same judgment.
—1 Corinthians 1:10

Our churches are to be embassies representing God's kingdom here on the earth. They are to be centers for creativity, art, innovation, and transformation. They are to be places where half-ideas meet one another to become whole; where diversity begets new levels of understanding; where pieces of the great puzzle of the mystery of Jesus Christ can find one another and connect. They are to be educational centers helping people to learn how to see as God sees. We enter and join our local churches as people seeking citizenship in a new kingdom, but we should leave equipped to be ambassadors and representatives of that kingdom in our workplaces, neighborhoods, and even our own homes.

Let me never be a spectator at church. Let me always be growing and contributing so my church becomes a center of transformation. Bring new levels of understanding and synergy so that Your body worldwide will walk in unity and become kingdom ambassadors who speak Your words and reveal Your will in the earth. In the name of Jesus, amen.

Push the Enemy Back

Proclaim this among the nations: "Prepare for war! Wake up the mighty men, let all the men of war draw near, let them come up. Beat your plowshares into swords and your pruning hooks into spears; let the weak say, 'I am strong.'"
—Joel 3:9–10

Destiny is God-given, God-revealed, and God-directed, or it is nothing. This is why we, the church, must renew our vigor and discipline in prayer. We must understand it anew. We have a world to transform, and we need God ideas to do it. The only way to get those will be to once again wear thin the veil between heaven and earth through prayer. We each have a part to play. We each have giftings, callings, abilities, skills, and talents God has uniquely given us to impact our jobs, communities, nations, and world. It is time to bring those to the battlefronts and start pushing the enemies back into the sea. It is time for more of us to stand up and take our places in the fight.

Father, direct me to my destiny. As I pray today, deposit Your ideas into my spirit. Use everything You have placed within my hands for Your glory. I am a soldier in Your army, and I push the enemy back to the sea. I declare and decree that I am strong in You, and I will boldly go wherever You lead me. In the name of Jesus, amen.

October 25

Take Your Place in Battle

So I sought for a man among them who would make a wall, and stand in the gap before Me on behalf of the land, that I should not destroy it; but I found no one.
—Ezekiel 22:30

Within our generation there is a need for us to step out from the shadows of timidity into the spotlight of moral and ethical leadership. There is a place for each of us in the fight between goodness and darkness on this planet. If we don't stand in our places on the battle lines, there will be gaps in our defenses, and all the authority of heaven will mean very little. Unexercised or unrealized authority is no authority at all. We need the right place to stand and apply God's Word in order to overturn the systems and syndicates that would keep our generation enslaved, impoverished, and subjugated.

I take my place in battle. I commit to bear Your light as an agent of change in a world of darkness. I decree and declare that there will be no gaps in my defenses. I will stand in the place I have been called to, in the authority I have been given through Christ, and pray diligently to release Your will in the earth. In the name of Jesus, amen.

Courage That Overcomes All Fear

God has not given us a spirit of fear, but of power and of love and of a sound mind.
—2 Timothy 1:7

The courage that overcomes all fear is the courage that is born of God, who places a divine overcoming, courageous gene within you by His Spirit. Look deeply within, and you will find the courage to step forward and take a stand. The Bible tells us, "You belong to God.... You have already won a victory...because the Spirit who lives in you is greater than the spirit who lives in the world" (1 John 4:4, NLT). It is manifested when you develop a healthy, realistic perspective of who you are in God and when you realize what He has wired you to do and to become.

I declare and decree today that fear has no place in my life. The righteous shall be as bold as lions, and He who is in me is greater than he that is in the world. Father, increase my awareness of who I am in You and what Your will is for my life. I know You have already equipped me to do exactly what You have called me to do. I will pursue my destiny without fear because You have called me and You are faithful to complete Your work in me. In the name of Jesus, amen.

October 27

Stand Firm in Your Position

Stand therefore...praying always with all prayer and supplication in the Spirit, being watchful to the end.
—Ephesians 6:14–18

The enemy will fight you in the area he fears you the most. To resist the temptation to wave the proverbial white flag signifying that you are giving up, take your stand in prayer. You will be equipped with the mind of Christ. Stand firm in your position as God's earthly representative. Be courageous. Courage will cause you to set plausible goals and dare to exceed the expectations of those who oppose you. Courage is what it takes to accomplish God's plans for your life.

I decree and declare that I am bold and courageous in You. I stand firm in my position as Your ambassador here on earth. I have been equipped with the mind of Christ, therefore I set achievable goals and exceed all expectations. I am strong and of good courage, and everything God has planned for my life will come to pass. In the name of Jesus, amen.

Face Your Fears

Do not let your heart envy sinners, but be zealous for the fear of the Lord all the day.
—Proverbs 23:17

Did you know that everyone is challenged at some point in their life's journey with some kind of fear? Even people whom we may perceive as not having any fear at all have had moments when they had to push past fear. The blessing does not lie in having no fear, because there is healthy fear—such as the fear of God. The blessing, however, lies in the efforts you make in working toward becoming mentally, emotionally, and spiritually strong and more skillful at what you are wired to do until you are empowered to face and conquer your fears.

In the name of Jesus I take authority over the spirit of fear. I declare and decree that it will have no effect on my life. I shall walk out of old, fearful ways of thinking and into a new mind-set that is filled with courage. I wear the helmet of salvation to protect my mind from negative thoughts that would derail Your purposes and plans for me. I am righteous and therefore am as bold as a lion. I decree and declare that I face and conquer every fear and advance into my destiny, in the name of Jesus. Amen.

Condition Your Mind

Fear not, for I am with you; be not dismayed, for I am your God. I will strengthen you, yes, I will help you, I will uphold you with My righteous right hand.
—Isaiah 41:10

God gave Joshua the encouragement he needed (Josh. 1:6), and he went on to become one of the most powerful commanders the nation of Israel ever had. He had to learn the art of conditioning his mind to succeed at life and to win. You too must learn the art of mental conditioning. Do not quit and give into your fears. Assume the posture of a conqueror.

Because You are with me, I will not give in to fear. You strengthen me, just as You strengthened Joshua, and You uphold me with Your hand. Everything I need to fulfill my kingdom assignment has already been provided. In the name of Jesus I break evil and inappropriate patterns in my mind. I declare and decree that I have a fresh mind that is fortified and resolute. No problem is bigger than You. I am a conqueror in You, and I will not quit until everything You have spoken over my life comes to pass. In the name of Jesus, amen.

Pray With Specificity

If you abide in Me, and My words abide in you, you will ask what you desire, and it shall be done for you.
—John 15:7

Prayer generals do more than just describe to God what He already knows. They actually unlock heaven's vault in order to unleash heaven's provisions. It is only after you make the request that spiritual helicopters and divine airplanes are deployed, loaded with supplies, and everything you need brought to that village. By praying with specificities, you can establish your own little bit of heaven on the earth right in the midst of a battle zone. Ask what you will, and it shall be done. That is exactly what you have been called to do wherever God has planted you. You must make your requests known unto God.

You have numbered every hair on my head; surely You are concerned about every detail of my life. I bring my specific requests to You because You long to give a specific response. According to Job 38, You provide food for ravens and direct the lion to her prey. The lightning bolts report to You. How much more do You care about my needs? I will not be afraid to bring all of my requests to You, because You delight in answering my prayer. Thank You for being so faithful to meet my needs. In the name of Jesus, amen.

October 31

Power vs. Authority

Behold, I give you the authority to trample on serpents and scorpions, and over the power of the enemy, and nothing shall by any means hurt you.
—Luke 10:19

One of the things we need to realize is that authority and power are different things, though we often use them interchangeably. The power is in the government or kingdom that backs the individual, but authority is invested in the individual as a representative of the government or kingdom. When kingdoms clash, the military with the superior training and equipment, the one with the most sophisticated arsenal and weaponry, will be the one to emerge as the ruling power. Our kingdom—the kingdom of heaven—has not only the power but also the authority to rule.

I decree and declare that I have authority to rule as Your ambassador on earth. By that authority, I command everything the enemy has swallowed up to be released. Every miracle, every blessing, every opportunity must be released now in the name of Jesus. By You, God, I run through troops; by You I leap over walls into new realms of power and authority. I live in the realm of unlimited possibilities. I will not cower; instead I establish my superior authority by the blood of Jesus. In Your name I pray, amen.

November

November 1

Prayer Is a Dialogue

He who is of God hears God's words.
—John 8:47

Prayer is first and foremost an essential way of opening communication with the throne room of God. You have probably heard that before, but I am hoping you will see it in a fuller light. Prayer is not a soliloquy but a dialogue. If it is not a two-way communication, it is not prayer—not that God doesn't hear, but if we are not open and patient enough to receive the answers and strategies He sends back to us, then what is the point of inquiring of God in the first place?

Father, I come before You today and listen for Your voice. Open my spiritual ears to hear You clearly. Create in me a heart that is receptive to the things of the spirit. Release heavenly downloads that give me prophetic discernment and direction today. I declare that You have free and unobstructed access to my mind and spirit. I thank You for being a God who hears and answers prayer. Thank You for renewing my strength as I spend time in Your presence. In the name of Jesus, amen.

November 2

Prayer Is Partnership

Your ears shall hear a word behind you, saying, "This is the way, walk in it," whenever you turn to the right hand or whenever you turn to the left.
—Isaiah 30:21

Prayer is not delegation. We don't give God a "to do" list and then sit back and wait for Him to take care of things. Prayer is a partnership. There are some things—such as cares, anxieties, and hurts—that we are to bring to the feet of Jesus and leave there for Him to handle. But there are also issues we bring to Jesus for Him to pour light into so we know what to do or say. We fast and pray that we might better pierce the veil between the spiritual and physical realms—that we would be stronger in the fruit and gifts of the Spirit so we are enabled to meet the needs of others when they come to us. We make ourselves the bridge of God's love and power to the earth. We dig into prayer, not that we would change God, but that He would change us.

Thank You for the privilege of partnering with You in prayer. Holy Spirit, You have permission to move in my life. Purify my heart. Remove every hindrance that would keep me from hearing You clearly today. Cause Your truth to pierce my understanding so I will know what to say and do. In Jesus's name, amen.

November 3

What Is Your Mission?

May God himself, the God who makes everything holy and whole, make you holy and whole, put you together—spirit, soul, and body—and keep you fit for the coming of our Master, Jesus Christ.
—1 Thessalonians 5:24, The Message

Wherever you are in the world right now—whatever "realms" you touch as you go through each week at church, at work, in the community, as a citizen of a nation and the world—God has missions and assignments He wants taken care of. Chances are, whatever touches your heart in what you see today also touches the heart of God. He wants to reach out into that place and fix things, but He needs hands to reach out—and that is the responsibility of His body. He is not just asking for a hand to reach out on His behalf and do *something*; He wants it to reach out and do *His thing.*

Father, I am Your hands and feet in the earth. Empower me to fulfill the mission You have assigned me today. Make me sensitive to the things that touch Your heart and show me just how You would have me to intervene. I declare and decree that I will not just do "something"; I will receive Your divine wisdom and do "Your thing" in Your perfect timing. In the name of Jesus, amen.

Synergy of Spirit and Word

All Scripture is given by inspiration of God, and is profitable for doctrine, for reproof, for correction, for instruction in righteousness.
—2 Timothy 3:16

The primary way God speaks to us is through His Word, and He never acts outside the practices and policies He has established in the Scriptures. Thus, meditating on the Scriptures is the check-and-balance system of our actions. We are people of the Spirit *and* the Word. It's not so much that they hold equal authority—it is more that they synergize each other. A person who understands his authority as outlined in the Word and confirmed by the Holy Spirit becomes more than the sum of the individual parts. It is much like the difference between the power of addition and the power of multiplication. The initial increments are not much different, but the further along you get, the curve starts skyrocketing almost straight up instead of each step along the way being the same increment as the step before.

I declare that I am a person of the Word and the Spirit. Because I neglect neither Your Word nor Your Spirit, my footing is firm and the power of God is at work in and through me. Thank You, Father, for equipping me to destroy the works of the enemy and advance Your kingdom agenda. In the name of Jesus, amen.

Get to Know God's Realm

For the word of God is living and powerful, and sharper than any two-edged sword, piercing even to the division of soul and spirit, and of joints and marrow, and is a discerner of the thoughts and intents of the heart.
—Hebrews 4:12

We must learn to see with our spiritual eyes as readily as we see with our physical eyes. We must come to understand how much greater God is than anything we could face here on the earth. We have to dig into the spirit in prayer so we are comfortable with God's realm and how it functions. And, of course, the Bible is our handbook for all things spiritual. It is spiritual food that strengthens and nurtures the human spirit within us. It is the personal trainer of the soul so that we can discern the thoughts and intents of the heart.

Father, sanctify me through Your Word. Bring my words into alignment with what heaven is saying about me today. Open my eyes to see spiritual realities. Allow me to ascend to new heights in You and walk in the realm of the supernatural, where the miraculous is commonplace. You are the only great and awesome God, and I stand in awe of You. Nothing I face today could ever compare with You. Father, order my steps in Your Word today. In the name of Jesus, amen.

November 6

Fortify Your Mind

That which is born of the flesh is flesh, and that which is born of the Spirit is spirit.
—John 3:6

It is one thing to understand the promise but another to allow the Word of God to fortify your mind so you have more confidence in the spiritual realm than you do in the physical. Too often we get overwhelmed because of what we see in the natural realm as opposed to the forces of God that are backing us up. The things of the spirit are eternal and unbeatable. We must learn how to delve into the unseen realm; it has resources we will never have access to in the natural, physical world.

Father, cause the supernatural realm to become more real to me than the natural. The supernatural realm is where change happens. Allow me to tap into the frequency of heaven and receive Your instructions for how I ought to pray today. Because whatever I loose in heaven will be loosed on earth, I command the enemy to release everything he has illegally held up and held back; he must let go of everything that belongs to me in Jesus's name. Father, I decree and declare that I will fulfill the mission You have for me today without hindrance. I have everything I need to accomplish Your will. In the name of Jesus, amen.

November 7

Present Your Case

"Come now, and let us reason together," says the Lord.
—Isaiah 1:18

The confidence, faith, and boldness with which you take your stand in prayer are critical to the presentation of your appeals and requests. Your communication in the Spirit with your Advocate, Jesus Christ, gives you revolutionary insight into how to correctly present your case and reason with God so you receive the answers and strategies you need.

I arise today in Your mighty strength and with the knowledge that I was born in this generation to contribute something significant. I am not here by accident. You have placed me here to fulfill Your purpose. Father God, let us reason together so I will know which strategy to employ to take the territory You are giving me. Let nothing prevent me from walking in the fullness of what You have for me. Let Your perfect will be done in and through me today. In the name of Jesus, amen.

Don't Limit Your Thinking

For by Him all things were created that are in heaven and that are on earth, visible and invisible.... All things were created through Him and for Him.
—Colossians 1:16

We have some work to do in the spirit. This kind of change doesn't happen overnight, but it happens gradually and progressively as we seek to understand the realm of the spiritual better than we understand the world we physically walk in every day. As we do, the transformation that is possible is beyond anything that has yet been imagined. We must not be limited by the thinking of the world around us. God has more, and He is anxious to release it into the earth, but He can do it only through His body. If it is going to happen, then it is going to come through us, and it is only going to come through us if we understand how to pray and hear from heaven in revolutionary new ways.

I decree and declare that I have the mind of Christ and therefore seek things above and not beneath. I ascend into new realms of power and access new dimensions of divine revelation. I declare that every mental block is cleared, giving the Holy Spirit unrestricted access to my mind, soul, and spirit. Father, reveal Your assignments and agenda for me today; I will operate in my correct timing. In the name of Jesus, amen.

Enforce Your Legal Authority

And David said with longing, "Oh, that someone would give me a drink of the water from the well of Bethlehem, which is by the gate!" So the three mighty men broke through the camp of the Philistines, drew water from the well of Bethlehem that was by the gate, and took it and brought it to David.
—2 Samuel 23:15–16

Many believers are desperate for a breakthrough, but breakthroughs have to be pursued. You must prevail over territorial spirits in order to possess your possessions. You must activate and exercise your dominion over a region within a realm, system, kingdom, industry, field, and discipline. David had a divine desire for that which God had prepared for him before the foundation of the world. The enemy had assumed squatter's rights until David enforced his legal authority over a region that belonged to him.

Father, place the anointing of a warrior upon me. Every domain and system that You have assigned me I confiscate from the enemy. I release the law of dispossession; every satanic or demonic squatter that is on my land, property, or territory I command to go in the name of Jesus. I am more than a conqueror. In the name of Jesus, amen.

Demand Restitution

The thief does not come except to steal, and to kill, and to destroy.
—John 10:10

The enemy has illegally seized many of our possessions and must be made to give them back—our reputations, our marriages, our children, our communities, our nations. He will not give them up until we demand it. We must learn how to pound at the gates of heaven through prayer and demand restitution for what he has stolen. He is a thief and must release what rightfully belongs to each of us.

I declare and decree that everything that pertains to my life and godliness and everything prepared for me before the foundation of the world must be released in its correct time and season. I command everything the enemy has swallowed up to be spat out and released. Let there be no demonic encroachment. Let there be no satanic squatters—in the name of Jesus get off my property, get off my territory, get out of my sphere of influence, get out of my family, get out of my relationships, get out of my finances, get out of my body, and get out of my mind. You must go now in the name of Jesus. Amen.

November 11

Prayer Isn't a Rulebook

Don't look for shortcuts to God.... The way to life—to God!—is vigorous and requires total attention.
—Matthew 7:13–14, The Message

A lot of people look for a rulebook for prayer. They want step one, two, three, and so on, so they don't have to think or pour that much of themselves into their prayers. They want to just check off the steps and feel they have done their duty. But prayer doesn't work like that. Battles don't work like that. While you may have a plan going into the fight, once you have made first contact with the enemy, everything changes. Will you stay the course even if people call you crazy? Will you let so much of yourself be invested in prayer that you feel as if you may die if you don't get what you are praying for? Desperate times call for desperate prayers.

Father, I pray not out of duty but because I am desperate for You, desperate for Your presence and power in my life. I cry out to You as David did. He cried out and You answered. Give me answers, Lord. Give me divine revelation and discernment to know what is on Your heart. Let my words bring life and liberty. I will not be deterred by what I see; I will persist in prayer until there is breakthrough. In the name of Jesus, amen.

Prayer Is Adaptation

David answered, "You come at me with sword and spear and battle-ax. I come at you in the name of God-of-the-Angel-Armies, the God of Israel's troops."
—1 Samuel 17:45, The Message

Prayer, like fighting on a battlefield, is often more about adaptation than it is about the soundness of the plan we take into it. It is more about cooperating and less about coercing. Will we allow God to change us once we get into the midst of the fight? It can mean the difference between success and failure. When you pray, you are often engaging the enemy of doubt, frustration, antagonism, and the disbelief hidden in the heart of others. They may not see what you are seeing—those things God shows you by revelation or places in your heart as a desire. In the heat of battle the wise general will read the field and adapt his original battle plan to match what he is seeing.

Father, help me to stay sensitive to Your voice today. Cleanse my heart of all carnality, rationalization, and hard-heartedness—anything that would keep me from following Your leading. I welcome Your revelation and divine insight. Cause my spiritual eyes to function with 20/20 vision for the correct understanding of the times and seasons. Father, as I cooperate with Your battle plan, anoint me for breakthrough. In the name of Jesus, amen.

November 13

Remain Flexible

We know that the Son of God has come and has given us an understanding, that we may know Him who is true.
—1 John 5:20

The zigzag is our metaphor for remaining flexible. You have to cooperate with the choreographic movement of the Spirit. In the heat of the battle you must learn how to discern the flow by listening to heaven's intelligence reports so you can understand the players involved, the spiritual terrain you must travel, as well as a myriad of other things. The general who wins is not always the one with the most apparent sophisticated battle plan going in but the one who adapts the best and responds effectively as the battle is taking place.

Father, help me to watch for Your movements and to cooperate with Your plans for me today. Make me sensitive to Your Spirit so I will hear Your divine intelligence report and know how to navigate this terrain in the spirit. Let Your supernatural wisdom and understanding be upon me today. Open my ears to hear the symphonic movements of the Spirit with clear, crisp transmission. Cause me to move in sync with Your perfect will for me, my family, my church, my work, and my community. In the name of Jesus, amen.

Make the World Better

For the kingdom of God is not in word but in power.
—1 Corinthians 4:20

I believe prayer is one of the most powerful contributions a Christian can give toward making this world a better place. You don't learn to pray powerfully and effectively by reading a how-to manual. You learn *how* to pray *when* you pray. When you do, you will discover there is no continent, no nation, no organization, no city, no office, no situation, no circumstance, no condition, no government, no case, no issue, and no battle that is off limits to the force of its effect. There is no person, no policy, nor any political power on this earth that can keep prayer out. Prayer is a game changer. Prayer makes a difference.

I am Your representative in the earth realm. I stand in the authority I have in You and command the spiritual climate to shift, the economic climate to shift, the social climate to shift, the political climate to shift, and the atmosphere around me to be filled with the glory of God. I declare and decree that the environment in my home, workplace, and region is suitable for my ministry, my family, my business, and my ideas to thrive and to be used to advance Your kingdom. In the name of Jesus, amen.

November 15

Prayer Creates Change

Embrace this God-life. Really embrace it, and nothing will be too much for you.... I urge you to pray for absolutely everything, ranging from small to large. Include everything as you embrace this God-life, and you'll get God's everything.
—Mark 11:22–24, The Message

If prayer was a sport, then it would be a contact sport. Prayer is the contact point between heaven and earth—or perhaps it is better said that the person who prays is that contact point. Your place of prayer is your place of power. Your place of prayer is your place of change management. We can create change through force of will and clever persuasion, but it won't last. Real, irrevocable change only comes through prayer.

Father, I commit to bear Your light as an agent of change in a world of darkness. I pray today with the confidence that You not only hear my prayers but also delight in answering them. Allow me to tap into in the realm of the supernatural so that I pray with divine insight and prophetic revelation. Father, open the heavens and pour out breakthrough. I will not abandon my post in prayer. I will persist in prayer until heaven invades earth. In the name of Jesus, amen.

Be Dedicated and Faith-Filled

God...gives life to the dead and calls those things which do not exist as though they did.
—Romans 4:17

When you pray, ensure that you do not waver in your faith. Hold fast to what you have learned and the confidence you have received in your relationship with Christ. God can resurrect a dead life, a dead dream—anything that is dead, if you have faith. If God can quicken the dead, He can bring your marriage, your business, your job, and your faith back into divine alignment with His promises. But most of the time this takes more than sending up a quick "Help me, God!" It takes dedicated, faithful, faith-filled prayer in which you present yourself to God ready to change and ready to do what He asks of you.

I prophesy today to the things that have died prematurely and dried up. I command them to quicken and come to life. I declare that the dead pieces of my purpose, destiny, finances, work, family, and ministry must come to life. Breathe new life into every hope that has died. Father, open up the floodgates of heaven and let it rain. Bring an end to spiritual, economic, and creative dryness and drought. Usher me into times of refreshing in the name of Jesus, amen.

November 17

Don't Waver

Let us hold fast the confession of our hope without wavering, for He who promised is faithful.
—Hebrews 10:23

You cannot be wishy-washy when you pray—one day you trust God, the next day you don't. One day you pray this, the next day you want the opposite. You say one thing to God in faith, and then you go have coffee with your friends and talk about how it can never happen. You are wishy-washy with what you want and where you are going. This cannot be so if you are to command your surroundings in the power of God.

In the name of Jesus I reject all forms of double-mindedness; it will not find a place in my life. I decree and declare that I receive only that which emanates from the mind of God, seeds of hope and faith. Father, cleanse my mind with Your Word. I decree and declare that like Daniel I will remain steadfast in prayer and faith and will not waver. In the name of Jesus, amen.

Agree With God's Word

If any of you lacks wisdom, let him ask of God, who gives to all liberally and without reproach, and it will be given to him. But let him ask in faith, with no doubting, for he who doubts is like a wave of the sea driven and tossed by the wind.
—James 1:5–7

Let there be no misunderstanding: you can speak words in prayer you don't believe, and they won't produce any result. Parroting something you have heard someone else say or read somewhere else without conviction doesn't produce divine alignment. Make a deliberate and conscious decision to agree with the Word of God, and then set your heart to believe it and your mouth to speak it no matter what.

I choose to agree with the Word of God, and I align my speech with what You are saying. Father, renew my mind with Your Word. Let it transform my heart and my speech. As I study Your Word, increase my faith and fill my mind with the knowledge of my true identity in You so I can exercise the authority and power You have given me. Thank You, Father, for giving me Your Word, for it is life and truth. In the name of Jesus, amen.

November 19

Seize What Belongs to You

The kingdom of heaven suffers violence, and the violent take it by force.
—Matthew 11:12

Don't be a wimp! You are not begging, you are not crying, and you are not persuading—you are coming to take what is legally yours according to the Word of God. You must come boldly as a child would to a father, as a prince or princess would to a king, as a wronged plaintiff would to a court of law.

Father, You have given me authority over all the power of the enemy. I walk in that authority today and decree that I possess my possessions and take them by force. Since my times are in Your hand, I declare and decree that my struggle is over. I decree sudden surprises, supernatural increase, favor, and influence. I declare that I am anointed for a new season. Old things are passed away; behold, all things are new. I am whole and strong, my heart is filled with peace, my mind is focused, and my life shines with Your glory. In the name of Jesus, amen.

You Don't Need to Beg

Without faith it is impossible to please Him, for he who comes to God must believe that He is, and that He is a rewarder of those who diligently seek Him.
—Hebrews 11:6

If you feel like you have to beg God for what He has promised, then you don't know the God of heaven. He is a rewarder. He isn't stingy in fulfilling His Word. But if you don't walk into His presence like you belong there, then your faith and understanding need an upgrade. It is not that you aren't humble; it's that you know God for the loving Father He really is.

I decree and declare a prophetic upgrading of my thought life; negative, self-defeating thought processes are under my feet. I now possess a kingdom paradigm, which grants me new ways of thinking, working, and living. I declare that new cycles of victory, success, and prosperity are replacing old cycles of failure, poverty, and death in my life. I decree that everything prepared for me before the foundation of the world must be released in Jesus's name. Thank You, Father, for crowning me with Your love and mercy. With all good things You satisfy me. In the name of Jesus, amen.

Pray Through the Eyes of God

As Moses lifted up the serpent in the wilderness, even so must the Son of Man be lifted up, that whoever believes in Him should not perish but have eternal life.
—John 3:14–15

We are not called to take vengeance on anyone—if vengeance is to be taken, it will be God taking it, not us. We are not called to be judges over the perpetrators of any wrongdoing. We are called to be rescuers and healers. We are called, like Moses when he lifted up the bronze serpent, to put ourselves between the people and the harm, lifting up Jesus so that those who will look up from this world to Him might also be saved. Because of this we must pray to see those who hurt us or the people we are praying for through the eyes of God. We must pray that God stops them in their tracks as He did Paul and turns them around. We cannot have faith for something if we are not walking in love, for the only thing that avails is "faith working through love" (Gal. 5:6).

Lord, give me supernatural wisdom to know how to pray for others. Help me to see them through Your eyes and to forgive those who have hurt me. I leave vengeance in Your hands. Empower me to lift You up today so people can look to You and be saved. In the name of Jesus, amen.

Seek the Truth

When He, the Spirit of truth, has come, He will guide you into all truth.
—John 16:13

There are times when we are honestly in denial about the truth of a situation, or we could just be mistaken about the facts or in how we are interpreting things. But one of the names of the Holy Spirit is "the Spirit of Truth." If we will open ourselves to Him in prayer and listen more than we speak, then there is room for the Holy Spirit to adjust our perspective. He will give us the perspective from the throne room of God that we would never get on our own.

Father, order my steps in Your Word and guide me into all truth. Let Your Word renew my mind and change my perspective. Then let the rest of my life fall in line so I exemplify the fruit of Your Spirit. As I diligently seek You and study Your Word, transform my life and my prayers. Help me to listen more and wait for revelation from Your throne so my prayers will be strategic and effective. In the name of Jesus, amen.

November 23

Pray the Truth

Jesus said to him, "I am the way, the truth, and the life."
—John 14:6, ESV

We don't necessarily need to be praying "the facts"—we need to be praying the truth. The facts might be that the doctor said you will die in six months, but the truth is "by His stripes we are healed" (Isa. 53:5). The facts may be that you have a lot of unpaid bills sitting on your desk, but the truth is "My God shall supply all your need according to His riches in glory by Christ Jesus" (Phil. 4:19). God doesn't need us to tell Him the facts—He knows them better than we do—but He does need us to agree with His promises so that we can receive the provision He desires to provide. After all, the Bible doesn't say, "You shall recognize the facts, and the facts will set you free," but it says, "You shall know the truth, and the truth shall make you free" (John 8:32).

Father, thank You for the truth that brings freedom. I believe Your Word over the facts of the situations I face. As I declare Your truth, my circumstances will change for the best. Thank You, Father, for making me victorious over every obstacle that comes my way today. In Jesus's name, amen.

You Can't Waste Prayer

Be steadfast, immovable, always abounding in the work of the Lord, knowing that your labor is not in vain in the Lord.
—1 Corinthians 15:58

Prayer is never wasted. I know from personal experience that one minute in prayer can accomplish more than a lifetime of other activities. Hold fast to God's promises in prayer no matter what things look like in the natural. God will answer you if you seek Him with all of your heart. (See Jeremiah 29:11–14.)

Father, I hold fast to Your promises. Though the vision tarry, I will wait for it, knowing that You will bring it to pass. Your Word declares that all of the promises of God are yes in You and amen, so I will persist in prayer until there is breakthrough. You are the one true God who makes everything work together and who works all things for good through Your most excellent harmonies. Thank You for faithfully hearing and answering prayer. In the name of Jesus, amen.

November 25

Let Passion Inform Your Prayers

Elijah was a man with a nature like ours, and he prayed earnestly that it would not rain; and it did not rain on the land for three years and six months. And he prayed again, and the heaven gave rain, and the earth produced its fruit.
—James 5:17–18

Life throws us curveballs, and though we have different backgrounds and personal histories, we all have emotions, dreams, and passions. When we are emotionally involved in a struggle, we tend to pray less rather than pray more. If we are to have overcoming prayer lives, we need to turn those emotions and passions into prayer rather than let them become a hindrance to it.

Father, cause my will to work in perfect harmony with Yours. You have put the seeds of transformation in my mouth. I will not let circumstances convince me that You are not able to meet my needs today. I will remind my circumstances of the greatness of my God. Like David, I will run to You in times of distress; I will not run away from You. My help comes only from You. Thank You for giving me an overriding sense of peace, love, mercy, favor, and the absolute assurance that You are in control. In the name of Jesus, amen.

November 26

Be Willing to Wrestle

Then Jacob was left alone; and a Man wrestled with him until the breaking of day.... And He said, "Let Me go, for day breaks." But [Jacob] said, "I will not let You go unless You bless me!"
—Genesis 32:24–26

Jacob had to wrestle with God to get His blessing. We have to come to God earnestly as who we are and be willing to stay in prayer—even if we are angry or frustrated—until we get God's answer. God understands emotions—He created them! We have to be willing to express them earnestly as much as we need to be ready for God to change or correct them.

Father, like Jacob, I won't let go of You until You bless me. I won't let go until change comes. I press through in prayer for a breakthrough. I need You, God. Without You I can do nothing. You are my only hope for the answers I seek. Help me to pray more, praise more, give more, believe more, and hope more. Give me a fortified mind that is stable and resolute and faith that is steadfast and unfaltering. Bring stability to my emotions. I praise You in advance for the great things You are going to do in and through me today. In the name of Jesus, amen.

November 27

In the Name of Jesus

Therefore God also has highly exalted Him and given Him the name which is above every name, that at the name of Jesus every knee should bow, of those in heaven, and of those on earth, and of those under the earth, and that every tongue should confess that Jesus Christ is Lord, to the glory of God the Father.
—Philippians 2:9–11

Praying in Jesus's name is not just a closing we are supposed to use before we say, "Amen." Praying in the name of Jesus is coming to the throne of God just as an ambassador would come to the throne of a foreign king "in the name of" his own king. Using the name of Jesus is another "in Christ" privilege and signet of our authority as a representative of Jesus. When we pray in the name of Jesus, we pray in the authority of Jesus. The name of Jesus will give you the power to overcome when you truly pray in that name.

I am Your ambassador, representing Your kingdom in the earth. I pray from a place of victory because You have already conquered the enemy. When I pray in Your name, according to Your Word, my request is as good as done. I just need to wait for it to manifest. Thank You, Father, for giving me authority in Your name—authority that empowers me to defeat the enemy and overcome every obstacle. In the name of Jesus, amen.

Your Road Is Unique

Are not two sparrows sold for a copper coin? And not one of them falls to the ground apart from your Father's will. But the very hairs of your head are all numbered. Do not fear therefore; you are of more value than many sparrows.
—Matthew 10:29–31

Just as each of us has a different calling or job to do for God, each of us will travel a slightly different road in understanding what prayer really is. God will speak to each of us in different ways, and the way God speaks to one person can be markedly different from the way He speaks to another. Why? Because God isn't interested in getting us to learn rules and requirements and living life merely by following the dictates of a rulebook. He wants us to come to Him that we might know Him for ourselves. He wants a unique relationship with each of us just as He created each of us as unique individuals. God is all about relationship, and the key to it is masterful prayer.

Father, I draw close to You through prayer. I listen for Your instructions and pray Your will into the earth. But the point of prayer is not merely to accomplish the mission I have been assigned but also to fellowship with You. Thank You for showing me my unique purpose as I spend time in Your presence. In the name of Jesus, amen.

November 29

Prayer Is Dynamic

Here's what I want you to do: Find a quiet, secluded place so you won't be tempted to role-play before God. Just be there as simply and honestly as you can manage. The focus will shift from you to God, and you will begin to sense his grace.
—Matthew 6:6, The Message

To a certain extent, learning to pray is a trial-and-error experience. On many levels prayer is as simple as opening our hearts to heaven and telling God how we feel, but it is also sublime. A lifetime spent in prayer will never be monotonous unless we pull back and stop growing in its practice. It is a unique journey God has designed for each of us. That is not to say that we can't learn about prayer from one another—otherwise what would be the point of my writing all of these books on it? But if all you do is read books, you will never really understand what prayer is all about. I can tell you, but you have to experience it for yourself to understand it.

Father, let me never complicate prayer or turn it into a religious ritual. My strength today comes from getting quiet before You, telling You what's on my heart, and then listening to hear what's on Yours. It's so simple, and yet it is the most important thing I will do today. Thank You, Father, for hearing and answering prayer. In the name of Jesus, amen.

Don't Stop Praying

Then He spoke a parable to them, that men always ought to pray and not lose heart.
—Luke 18:1

You can never, never, never let prayer become a stagnant part of your life. It is vital to who you are as a Christian and even more vital to fulfilling God's mission and your assignment upon the earth. There is nothing more pleasing to the devil than a Christian who doesn't pray, because that person is someone he doesn't have to waste his time worrying about. In fact, his overall strategy over the years seems to be to get us too busy to pray and for us to think that we don't really need to pray because God already knows our needs, so why bother Him with them by praying? However, John Wesley famously said, "I pray two hours every morning. That is if I don't have a lot to do. If I have a lot to do for that day, then I pray three hours."

Renew my zeal today to seek You daily in prayer. Place upon me Deborah's anointing for balance so I never cram so much into my day that I don't leave time for You. It is Your will that I pray always because this is how You prepare me for the challenges I will face. You move mountains when I pray, so I won't stop. I will seek You first. In the name of Jesus, amen.

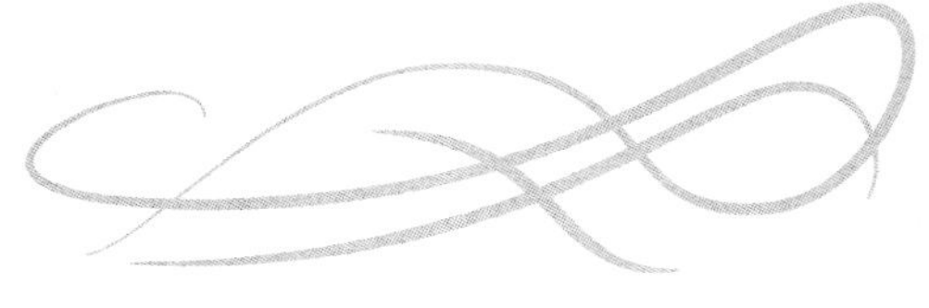

December

December 1

Establish the Kingdom

Let justice roll down like waters, and righteousness like an ever-flowing stream.
—Amos 5:24, esv

It is not enough to glimpse the kingdom in the distance and rush to slide under the gate just in time before it comes crashing down; we must press in and see the kingdom established wherever we go. Salvation is not a one-time decision that guarantees heaven, but it's a lifetime of releasing justice into our world on all levels. If we are going to live by Christ's commandment to love one another, justice is going to be our business at all levels. And nothing brings down justice like establishing the kingdom of God in a place.

Father, let Your kingdom come and Your will be done. Show me the cause that I am assigned to champion. Give me the courage to rally others around plausible goals for social reconstruction, community development, spiritual renewal, economic empowerment, and educational reformation. Father, remove self-serving leaders and replace them with true servant-leaders. Let the body of Christ live true to our biblical principles. Shift the spiritual climate in support of a move of God, and let us reclaim lost territory for You. In the name of Jesus, amen.

Get God's Downloads

Now the word of the Lord came to me, saying, "Before I formed you in the womb I knew you, and before you were born I consecrated you; I appointed you a prophet to the nations."
—Jeremiah 1:4–5, esv

Each one of us has been given industry-specific assignments that can only be effectively and efficiently discharged once bathed in prayer. As God makes more of Himself available, those who hear from heaven best will be in on the most incredible things! We will accomplish great exploits in His name until the kingdoms of this world become the kingdom of our Lord and of His Christ—until He reigns forever and ever. We must remind God of His Word, download God's plans and tactics, and claim His promises for this generation.

Father, clear away any distractions that would keep me from hearing You clearly today. Let me hear from heaven and pray with discernment. Give me prophetic insight into the things You have prepared for me today and the assignment I am to fulfill. I long to do great exploits that glorify Your name and promote and propel Your kingdom. I claim all of Your promises for my life in the name of Jesus. Amen.

December 3

Be Ready for God's Day

For the day of the Lord is near upon all the nations. As you have done, so shall it be done to you; your deeds shall return on your own head.
—Obadiah 15, esv

As the day of the Lord draws nearer, we need to draw nearer to Him as well. It will be an exciting time to be on the earth, and I believe we are to get ready for it by doing our part right where we are today. It is time to pray, fast, obey, and display the power of God. And that all starts with you digging in and fighting the battle you have right in front of you right now. Heaven already has the plans for your victory—it's time to download them and walk them out.

Father, You are near to everyone who calls on You, so I know You are near me today. I seek the wisdom of heaven so I will know both how to live and how to pray. I long to do Your will. Cause me to walk in sync with Your perfect timing. Bring everything that is misaligned into divine alignment. And release everything prepared for me before the foundation of the world in its correct time and season. Thank You for already having plans for my success. I praise You in advance for giving the victory. In the name of Jesus, amen.

December 4

Never Compromise

"No weapon formed against you shall prosper, and every tongue which rises against you in judgment you shall condemn. This is the heritage of the servants of the Lord, and their righteousness is from Me," says the Lord.
—Isaiah 54:17

Just as Daniel prospered through prayer despite persecution and trials within his sphere of influence that drew the proverbial line in the sand of justice, and just as Jesus advanced the kingdom through deliberately living in such a way that His life transformed people, may you neither bow your knees to the god of this world nor compromise your convictions as God promotes and prospers you. Remember, as God makes you the head and not the tail—an industry leader, trendsetter, and an agent of change—and as you commit to develop a life of prayer, refuse to preserve the status quo.

Father, I will not compromise. Like Daniel, I will be known as someone who exemplifies integrity, morality, and credibility. Your Word illuminates my path. Father, syncopate my actions and activities to heaven's rhythm today. As I spend time with You in prayer, give me the courage to walk out my convictions and the wisdom to impact my spheres of influence. In the name of Jesus, amen.

December 5

God Will Exalt You

So humble yourselves under the mighty power of God, and at the right time he will lift you up in honor.
—1 Peter 5:6, nlt

Using doctrine or tradition to hold one group of people down for the betterment of another is not God's method of operation. God is an empowerer. He wants to take the weak and lowly, the humble and meek, and see them exalted. If He brings down the proud, it is only because He wants to be the exalter and not see them exalt themselves to their own demise. His way is to maximize the potential of every person who will come to Him. He wants every person to become all she or he can be according to His original plan for each one. If we are going to be like Him and make a difference on the earth, we need to operate in the same way.

Father, empower me to maximize my potential today. As I walk humbly before You, cause me to ascend into new territory, realms, and dimensions. Open doors no man could open and close doors no man could shut. Show me how to use the gifts and resources You have given me to campaign for others' empowerment. Give me divine opportunities to help others succeed and become all You have called them to be. In the name of Jesus, amen.

Establish the Justice of God

The creation itself also will be delivered from the bondage of corruption into the glorious liberty of the children of God. For we know that the whole creation groans and labors with birth pangs together until now.
—Romans 8:21–22

The world was not built as a place that could handle the corruption that comes from sin. Even the earth itself groans with earthquakes and calamities, hoping for righteousness to be established on the earth. As things grow darker, the earth cries out all the more for the justice of God to be established.

Father, let the earth be filled with Your glory. Creation groans for the children of God to be revealed. Use me to establish Your righteousness and justice in the earth today. Cause the spiritual atmosphere to shift and become conducive for revival. Let me walk before You with integrity, honoring You with my words and my actions. I declare and decree that I live true to biblical principles and my name is associated with honesty, humility, grace, joy, peace, generosity, and wisdom. Through You I make a difference in the world around me. In the name of Jesus, amen.

December 7

Be the One Faithful Soul

Surely the Lord God does nothing, unless He reveals His secret to His servants the prophets.
—Amos 3:7

We see that God will spare a city or even an entire nation for the sake of one faithful soul who will stand in the gap on their behalf. In our age, that means God is looking for those on earth who are listening for heaven's instructions on what needs to be prayed for, who needs to be interceded for, and what needs to be prayed away before it happens. When there is no intercessor willing to stand in the gap and pray until heaven's righteousness can overcome the earth's corruption, something real and tangible—with the potential to make a kingdom difference—is lost.

Father, I will not forsake my post. I will stand in the gap to bring Your righteousness to bear on the corruption in the earth. Give me heavenly downloads today so I will know just how to pray. Open my eyes and ears to the things on Your heart. For this reason was the Son of God made manifest, that He would destroy the works of the devil. Use me to manifest Your glory in the earth and cause Your plans and purposes to prevail. In the name of Jesus, amen.

Fight the Good Fight

David replied to the Philistine, "You come to me with sword, spear, and javelin, but I come to you in the name of the Lord of Heaven's Armies.... Today the Lord will conquer you."
—1 Samuel 17:45–46, NLT

For a community to flourish, evil must be continually defeated—day after day, year after year, generation after generation. Otherwise all that happens is continual strife and infighting. Many people have become disillusioned because they feel it is a never-ending battle. But you must take heart; do not be discouraged. The battle we are engaged in will end in victory. Therefore, you must fight the good fight of faith and not of doubt. You must not give in to disbelief.

Father, I speak to my spirit and declare that I will persist in prayer. I will fight the good fight of faith and not give up. I am already victorious in You; I am more than a conqueror. I reject and repel all doubt and disbelief. I declare that I walk by faith and my speech is guided by Your Word. Let every scheme to frustrate Your plans and purposes be exposed and demolished. I decree and declare that no weapon formed against me will prosper because the Lord of Heaven's Armies has already defeated the enemy. In the name of Jesus, amen.

December 9

Fight to Win

Yet in all these things we are more than conquerors through Him who loved us.
—Romans 8:37

God's power and goodness that are within are far more powerful than any evil without. Conquer the foes of doubt and unbelief within, and your enemies without will be vanquished. You will win over personal stumbling blocks, proclivities, habits, and addictions in your private life, and you will win over the struggle against injustice around the world. We long for God's will—His mercy, His salvation, His healing, His abundance—to be done on the earth just as it is in heaven. We must fight to win. This is our war.

Father, I declare today that Your power and goodness are greater than all the internal battles I face. Your perfect love casts out fear. Your grace covers my sin. Because of Your loving-kindness I am not overwhelmed. Nothing can separate me from Your love. Let every trace of doubt and unbelief be exposed and cast out. Reveal every area that I have not trusted You with—every habit, proclivity, or addiction—so I can bring it under Your authority. Let Your will be done in my life as it is in heaven. I long to reflect Your glory. Make me more like You in the name of Jesus. Amen.

Nothing Is Beyond Imagining

For the weapons of our warfare are not of the flesh but have divine power to destroy strongholds. We destroy arguments and every lofty opinion raised against the knowledge of God.
—2 Corinthians 10:4–5, esv

It is in prayer that we probe spiritual realities, communicate with God, access the arsenal of heaven, and expand God's kingdom on the earth. It is as simple as pulling aside to a quiet place and opening your heart to God and as dynamic as tapping into the power and imagination that created the cosmos. As with God, nothing is impossible, so it is that through prayer, nothing is implausible. Prayer gives heaven permission to invade the earth. Through this discipline we are able to pray heaven down to keep hell from rising.

Father, let heaven invade earth and bring mind-blowing change. With You, nothing is impossible, so I will not put limits on my thinking about what You will and won't do. I take the barriers off and raise my level of expectation today. You are the great and mighty God, who is capable of doing more than I could ask or think. I decree and declare that every situation and circumstance in my life today must give way to the power and purpose of God. In the name of Jesus, amen.

December 11

Let God Release His Power Through You

Nor will they say, "Look, here it is!" or "There!" for behold, the kingdom of God is in the midst of you.
—Luke 17:21, ESV

God is right here with you, living inside of you, ready to release His kingdom through you. Every believer is equipped with an arsenal of incredible life-altering and world-changing power. For those who rightly esteem the privilege of accessing God's armory of possibilities, each word spoken through or by that person holds enormous. innovative, potential creative and re-creative power.

I decree and declare today that I am anointed for this time and season. I have been empowered by the Holy Spirit to pray with authority and to fulfill my destiny. Spirit of God, I release You to move freely in my life. I decree and declare that I see no impossibilities. I see only more chances for You to show Your strength on my behalf. In the name of Jesus, amen.

God Will Sustain It

The heart of man plans his way, but
the Lord establishes his steps.
—Proverbs 16:9, esv

Whatever God births through you in prayer, He is also required to sustain. You see, it doesn't matter what human beings formulate, plan, and strategize upon the earth, for all of it will ultimately come to nothing. God is a big God who created a big world for you to do something big in it. He is always trying to communicate with you. Prayer is the means by which you can engage Him.

You are faithful, God. You called me, and You will complete the work You called me to do. Nothing is too hard for You. Even things beyond my wildest dreams are easy for You. I decree and declare that You who made the earth by Your power, who established the world by Your wisdom and stretched out the heavens by Your understanding are ordering my steps today to fulfill Your purposes. You are a big God with big plans for me, and I will walk in all You have for me. I declare that You are tearing down every Jericho wall so I can possess the territory You have prepared for me. In the name of Jesus, amen.

Listen to God's Conversation

You have done all these things, declares the Lord, and when I spoke to you persistently you did not listen, and when I called you, you did not answer.
—Jeremiah 7:13, esv

Right now there is a big conversation going on, and God is sharing some big ideas. You need to get in on the big conversation going on in heaven's war room right now. God is always speaking. Are you listening? If you participate in prayer correctly, consistently, faithfully, and persistently, God will let you listen in on that conversation, and you will overhear exactly what it is you need to do to continually advance in your life, fulfill your purpose, and maximize your potential.

Father, I incline my ear to hear Your voice. I long to be in on the big conversation taking place in heaven. I humbly ask that You allow me to ascend into new realms of authority and access new dimensions of divine revelation so I will know how I ought to pray. Clear the lines of communication so You have unrestricted access to my mind and spirit. Let Your divine instructions flow freely today, and cause me to walk in Your perfect will. In the name of Jesus, amen.

Keep Maturing

Do not be children in your thinking. Be infants in evil, but in your thinking be mature.
—1 Corinthians 14:20, esv

We must grow up and mature in our faith if we are to make any difference for the kingdom of God. As we grow in Christ, we learn new skills and develop divine habits. Our levels of proficiency increase in our abilities and talents. We are distinguished by the excellence achieved and seeming ease with which we follow Jesus. Mastery of skills and techniques in any endeavor sets you apart as someone who is not casual in your pursuit.

Father, I choose to grow up in You. I refuse to allow any expression of childishness or immaturity to rob me of moving into new realms in the spirit. I submit to Your superior authority in my life, and I will not reject the process by which You are sharpening the skills and talents You have given me. Everything I have comes from You, and I freely give it back to You to use for Your glory. I do not seek You casually; I am in relentless pursuit of You. I openly embrace all of Your training in order to grow into the fullness of maturity in Christ. In Jesus's name, amen.

December 15

You Live in the Spiritual Realm

And God said to them, "Be fruitful and multiply and fill the earth and subdue it, and have dominion over the fish of the sea and over the birds of the heavens and over every living thing."
—Genesis 1:28, esv

In the kingdom of heaven the believer's earthly experience is filled with the essence of the righteousness that is God. It is a spiritual realm in which believers are privileged to exist and function at prosperous levels while physically living in the earth. This life is lived with the perspective originally intended by God at the forefront—that is, fulfilling God's original mandate to humanity—that we are to have dominion on the earth.

Father God, I will not limit my expectations to what I can see in the natural. My life is hid in You. I exist in a supernatural realm that defies natural limitations. I receive the added things that come with being a citizen of the kingdom of God. I decree and declare that the works of my hand are blessed. My life is blessed. Joy, peace, prosperity, success, and influence are my constant companions. You created me to have dominion. That is my kingdom mandate, and I will walk in it. Father, empower me to maintain a kingdom perspective. In the name of Jesus, amen.

Prayer Trains You

Blessed is the man whom you discipline, O Lord, and whom you teach out of your law, to give rest from days of trouble.
—Psalm 94:12–13, esv

God planted it within each of us to want to make a difference in our world—a difference that will bring good and not harm, peace and not strife, prosperity and not poverty. But too few realize the groundwork for this overcoming lifestyle begins in our prayer closets. It is the place of training and preparation. It is the boot camp to overcoming. Just as one who is not practiced in the art of swordcraft cannot artfully wield a sword, no person on this earth can correctly use God's Word who has not been trained in it by the Master Himself. Prayer is that place of training, and also the place of overcoming.

Father God, deepen my understanding of Your Word today. Let it cleanse my heart and renew my mind. Your Word is a two-edged sword that divides soul from spirit and discerns the intents of the heart. It is a lamp unto my feet that illuminates the path I should walk. Because I love truth, I discipline myself to study Your Word and submit myself to Your boot camp to overcoming. In the name of Jesus, amen.

Allow God to Discipline You

For the moment all discipline seems painful rather than pleasant, but later it yields the peaceful fruit of righteousness to those who have been trained by it.
—Hebrews 12:11, ESV

While we as Christians have all the power behind us, how well are we acting in that authority? We are overcomers, but are we overcoming? The determination in whether we will be victorious or defeated hangs upon honest answers to these questions. Thus, the issue is not the power of our God, but how disciplined and prepared we are to win the battles of our spiritual war in prayer.

Father, in the name of Jesus I declare and decree today that I do not just talk about the authority I have in You; I also walk in it. I proclaim the King and Your kingdom, and I walk in Your power. I take dominion over this day and declare that it shall cooperate with Your agenda and calendar. I cancel all destiny-altering activity in the name of Jesus. I have been given authority over all the power of the enemy, and I decree that my life is characterized by liberty. Train my hands for war. Bring me to new levels of power and authority as I submit myself to You. In the name of Jesus, amen.

You Need to Fight

Therefore submit to God. Resist the devil and he will flee from you.
—James 4:7

While the victory is ever the Lord's, it will not manifest on the earth if you as a believer do not fight for it. This is your time on the earth to see that God's will is done during your watch. You, who have jurisdiction on the earth while you are here, must stand in the gap and tell Satan, "No, I will have none of your monkey business here." Praying earnestly—and ultimately victoriously—in such matters is to strive in the spirit through mastery of the techniques and disciplines of prayer.

I arise today and declare like the prophet Isaiah that a Child has been born unto us, a Son has been given, and the government shall be upon His shoulder; of the increase of His government and peace there shall be no end. As an ambassador of that kingdom, I persist in prayer until every impenetrable wall comes down, until every barrier, blockage, and boulder hindering the purposes of God for this day is shattered. I will advance the cause of Christ. I decree and declare that the King and His kingdom are here, and His will shall be done in the earth as it is in heaven, in the name of Jesus, amen.

December 19

Pray Persistently

But if we hope for what we do not see, we wait for it with patience.
—Romans 8:25, esv

At the moment a prayer is uttered, angelic hosts move throughout the atmospheres on behalf of the pray-ers, rooting up and tearing down entrenched strongholds that have wreaked havoc on lives. Then God meticulously plants and nurtures, one by one, the answers to counteract those evils, until all is in alignment with His will. Just as it took a long time for the enemy to spawn his diabolical webs and trap people in them, it will take time as well to unravel and reposition people to receive the blessings of the Lord. Therefore, we must pray patiently, persistently, and passionately. Staying steadfast in prayer over such matters until the answer arrives not only is the key to victory, but it also matures our faith in ways that no other practice can.

Father, I thank You that the effectual, fervent prayers of the righteous avail much. I will continue in prayer until I see the manifestation of Your promises. As I pray, release Your angelic hosts to war on my behalf. Assign them to reinforce me as I advance into new levels, dimensions, realms, and territories to promote and propel Your kingdom. In the name of Jesus, amen.

Receive Divine Strategies

This is how one should regard us, as servants of Christ and stewards of the mysteries of God.
—1 Corinthians 4:1, esv

When we spend consistent and fervent time in prayer, knowing God, discerning His voice, and walking in His ways become as intimate to us as knowing those who live with us in our homes. It opens us to understanding the mysteries of God and allows God to reveal to us exact strategies for praying for specific people, growing our churches, changing our communities, and releasing God's kingdom on the earth. It also lets God's wisdom rub off on us regarding how to conduct our businesses, how to invest and manage our money, what we need to do to nurture our relationships, and how to discipline ourselves to keep our bodies fit and strong.

Father, as I spend time with You, shape my attitude and actions to reflect Your character. Reveal supernatural strategies for success, spiritual growth, good health, and prosperity. Give me new ways of living. Upgrade my thinking with kingdom technology and kingdom methodology to accomplish Your will. I receive the supernatural discipline to implement them today. Make me more like You. In the name of Jesus, amen.

December 21

It Takes Commitment

Do not fear what you are about to suffer.... Be faithful to death, and I will give you the crown of life.
—Revelation 2:10, esv

Making your mark in the world as someone who prays is hard. If it were easy, everybody would do it. But it takes patience, it takes commitment, and it comes with plenty of failures along the way. The real test is not whether you avoid the failures or not, because you won't. It is whether you allow them to discourage you and cause you to resign to a place of inactivity.

I declare that I am more than a conqueror. Father, shield me today from discouragement and sabotage. I decree and declare that I will not give up in the face of hardship. I will pray fervently and consistently, and You will show Yourself strong in my life. In the name of Jesus, amen.

Sit and Wait

[Martha] had a sister called Mary, who also sat at Jesus' feet and heard His word.... And Jesus answered and said to her, "Martha, Martha, you are worried and troubled about many things. But one thing is needed, and Mary has chosen that good part, which will not be taken away from her."

—Luke 10:39–42

So much of the time I see Christians running from one meeting to another trying to get the best teaching possible—and there is a great deal of good teaching out there—but at the same time I see Jesus standing in the back of these same meetings watching and wondering when they are going to come and spend some time learning at His feet. They're like God's paparazzi, running around and hoping to catch a glimpse of some great thing or person, hoping to cash in on being in the right place at the right time, but with no discipline to take the time to wait on God for themselves.

Father, I sit at Your feet today and listen for Your voice. You long to speak to me. I learn from You in Your presence. I gain strength in Your presence. My perspective is changed in Your presence. Let me ascend to higher heights; take me into deeper depths in the name of Jesus. Nothing I desire compares with You. Amen.

Wait for the Set Time

Now faith is the substance of things hoped for, the evidence of things not seen.
—Hebrews 11:1

We have the right to establish things in the spirit and begin to make a demand on things that have been divinely incubating, awaiting their set time of manifestation. It takes faith to fight for such manifestations. Since the beginning of the earth God prepared to answer what you have only asked for now. These answers have a set time of manifestation. But they can only be released by faith. Natural eyes cannot perceive them, nor can natural ears detect them. They must be discerned by the spirit and activated by faith.

Father, I put a demand on heaven today and call for everything reserved for me to be released in its correct time and season. Everything prepared for me before the foundation of the world must be loosed. I command everything the enemy has illegally held up to be released now in the name of Jesus. My family, finances, breakthrough, and miracles must be loosed. There will be no substitutes, no holdups, no setbacks, and no delays in the name of Jesus. Amen.

Are You a Prayer General?

We are of God. He who knows God hears us; he who is not of God does not hear us. By this we know the spirit of truth and the spirit of error.
—1 John 4:6–7

A prayer general prays until he or she sees results. Such prayer warriors have earned their stripes through seeing battles to their victorious end. These are people who can recognize the voice of God, know how to download the strategies of heaven, and can successfully implement them until the expected results are achieved. This is the person who not only prays with the same regularity as he or she breathes, but also when he or she takes your hand to pray in agreement with you, you sense the Spirit of God engulfing you like a warm fog. These are the people who speak with such an anointing that their words hit like punches to your stomach if they are words of correction or like refreshing nectar if they are words of encouragement.

Father, as I spend time with You in prayer, deepen my understanding of spiritual realities. Take me to new realms in the spirit and anoint me for breakthrough. Give me discernment to know truth from error and Your voice from my own reasoning so that my prayers go forth like missiles and knock evil out of its place. In the name of Jesus, amen.

December 25

Ambassadors of Hope

For there is born to you this day in the city of David a Savior, who is Christ the Lord. And this will be the sign to you: You will find a Babe wrapped in swaddling cloths, lying in a manger.
—Luke 2:11–12

God sent His greatest gift to mankind when He gave us Jesus. Born in a manger and wrapped in swaddling cloths, Jesus didn't look anything like a king. But the greatness wrapped up in an unassuming package would change the world as we know it. He brought light and hope to a world in crisis, and He wants us to do the same. As God's ambassadors in the earth, we are called to showcase His glory in our every interaction. The world is still in crisis; it is still in need of the hope Jesus came to bring. Now is the time for you to tap into the greatness wrapped inside you and become God's change agent in the earth.

Father, thank You for sending Your Son to save me from my sins. I decree and declare today that I am Your change agent in the earth. You have equipped me with unique gifts and talents, and I will use them to proclaim Your kingdom. I will not shirk my responsibility to be an ambassador of Your light and hope. I will walk in the authority I have been given through Christ and allow You to showcase Your love and power through me. In the name of Jesus, amen.

Trust God's Outcome

Father, if it is Your will, take this cup away from Me; nevertheless not My will, but Yours, be done.
—Luke 22:42

Many people want to pray as if they could actually push God to do or not do what is in His providence to do. The truth is, we have entered God's rest when we give up ownership of the matter. Rest assured, God always answers our prayers. The outcome may not be what you planned, but the result will be far greater than your heart could have conceived. You must also trust God to know what answer is in your best interest.

Father, I rest in the assurance that You are in complete control. I trust You with the outcome of my prayers. Answer my requests according to Your perfect will, not mine. I know Your way is always best. I bring my requests before You, and I do not worry because the peace of God that passes all understanding guards my heart and mind. Thank You, Father, for allowing me to enter into Your rest. I put my confidence in You. In the name of Jesus, amen.

December 27

Never Give Up

Therefore, my beloved brethren, be steadfast, immovable, always abounding in the work of the Lord, knowing that your labor is not in vain in the Lord.
—1 Corinthians 15:58

In your communication to, with, and on behalf of God, plant your feet wide apart in the spirit realm, stake your claim, be steadfast and unmovable, and defy any and all circumstances to move you from your position in prayer. In the days when God is extracting sins and evil and replanting with salvation, we may not see any evidence above the ground that He is at work beneath the soil. Yet we cannot afford to stop praying just as the results are about to break forth. The seedling will need your steadfastness in order to push through and flourish. Do not give up. Push; persevere. Never, never give up or give in. It's time to be steadfast and wait on the Lord. God, in whom you put your trust, is always faithful to answer.

I decree and declare that I am steadfast and immovable, always abounding in the work of the Lord, knowing that my labor is not in vain. Everything preventing my breakthrough must give way to the power and purpose of God. I decree and declare that my breakthrough is on its way, and I will prevail in prayer until the answer springs forth. In Jesus's name, amen.

You Are Heaven's Ambassador

As they heard these things, He spoke another parable, because He was near Jerusalem and because they thought the kingdom of God would appear immediately.
—Luke 19:11

Heaven's desire is for God's kingdom to be restored upon the earth, but heaven needs representatives and ambassadors on the earth to give it a legitimate right to step in and set up jurisdiction. It is only through our appeals—our prayers—that heaven gains the right to inhabit the earth. In other words, prayer legalizes heaven's interventions.

I decree and declare that the kingdom of the world shall become the kingdom of our Lord and of His Messiah, and He will reign for ever and ever. Father, reveal Your will to me in prayer and use me to make it a reality in the earth. Put Your Word in my mouth so my speech aligns with Your plans and purposes. Empower me to represent You well in my dealings today and to live true to Your principles. Let my life reflect Your glory and divinity. In the name of Jesus, amen.

December 29

Fight for It

I have set before you life and death, blessing and cursing; therefore choose life, that both you and your descendants may live.
—Deuteronomy 30:19

The earth is the domain of decisions. It is where human beings have the right to choose good or evil, blessing or cursing, success or failure, life or death. But these things don't just come with the choosing—they must also be fought for. For the earth is also the place of battles and wars, defeat and victory, abundance and need, risk and reward, and prosperity and calamity. We must realize that being on the earth means we live in the heart of the war zone between heaven and hell, good and evil, eternal life and eternal death. It is our place of testing and struggle, but it's also the only place we can experience victory and earn reward—although neither will come without a fight.

In the name of Jesus I declare that my spirit man is clad with the armor of the Lord and the armor of light. I have the mind of Christ; every stronghold is broken off my mind, and divine inspiration and wisdom flow freely. I take every territory that has been assigned to me. Nothing will hinder the plans and purposes of God for my life. Father, I praise You for making me more than a conqueror in the name of Jesus, amen.

Receive Your Instructions

He said, "My Presence will go with you, and I will give you rest."
—Exodus 33:14

You read the Bible to understand God's laws, the history of His people, and His nature. His revelation, however, comes from His presence, which you experience primarily through prayer. It is only through prayer that you receive revelation that is particular to you as an individual. It is through prayer you receive the specific instructions and stratagems to fight the battles in your part of the overall war for righteousness on the earth. It is through prayer God gives a fresh word specific to your current situations and reveals to you where you are in His plan for your life.

Father, You delight in the details. You have numbered the hairs of my head. You collect my every tear. You know every concern before I even bring it to You in prayer. You have a specific strategy for this day and a clear plan for my life and my future. Reveal Your instructions as I wait in Your presence. Give me a fresh word for this day, a unique strategy from heaven, so I can accomplish all You have for me. In the name of Jesus, amen.

December 31

You Are a Resistance Fighter

For we do not wrestle against flesh and blood.... Therefore take up the whole armor of God, that you may be able to withstand in the evil day.

—Ephesians 6:12–13

Within the world system you are considered a resistance fighter. Your mission is to join the prayer resistance force and return the earth to its original ownership and rulership. You have been chosen to follow Christ and to reestablish the kingdom of heaven—and then expand its borders as far as you can make them reach. It is not a task you can do alone, though. You must join with others of like mind and like precious faith. This is a revolution that most likely will not be broadcast on the nightly news. You most likely will not gain much attention or receive the accolades befitting a hero. But you must take the challenge to become God's hero. God will not force you to do it. You must make a decision.

I take my place in battle and declare that the King and His kingdom have come. The light of Your presence and power shall overtake the darkness. I decree and declare that nothing shall hinder God's will in my life and in the earth; the original plans and purposes of God for my life, my family, and my generation shall prevail. In the name of Jesus, amen.

Notes

February

1. ThinkExist.com, "Albert Einstein Quotes," http://thinkexist.com/quotation/i_am_enough_of_an_artist_to_draw_freely_upon_my/12640.html (accessed August 30, 2013).
2. James Allen, *As a Man Thinketh* (New York: Cosimo, Inc., 2005), 26.
3. ThinkExist.com, "Henry David Thoreau Quotes," http://thinkexist.com/quotation/go_confidently_in_the_direction_of_your_dreams/7805.html (accessed August 30, 2013).
4. As quoted in John Foppe *What's Your Excuse?* (Nashville: Thomas Nelson, 2002).

July

1. Brother Lawrence, *The Practice of the Presence of God: The Best Rule of Holy Life* (Peabody, MA: Hendrickson Publishers, 2004), ix.